SILVER BURDETT & GINN
English

Nancy Nickell Ragno • Marian Davies Toth • Betty G. Gray
Myra Cohn Livingston, Poetry Author

SILVER BURDETT & GINN

MORRISTOWN, NJ • NEEDHAM, MA

Atlanta, GA • Cincinnati, OH • Dallas, TX • Menlo Park, CA • Northfield, IL

Acknowledgments

Cover: © ZEFA/Photo Researchers, Inc.

Contributing Artists: Karen Ackoff, Michael Adams, Mary Alice Baer, Lisa Bailey, Bill Bell, Deborah Borgo, Penny Carter, Eulala Connor, Rick Cooley, Carolyn Croll, Marie DeJohn, Robin Eaton, Len Ebert, Michele Epstein, Carolyn Ewing, Lori Farbanish, Pamela Ford-Johnson, Peggy Frase, Kathleen Garry-McCord, Joan Goodman, Nancy Hannons, Paul Harvey, Meryl Henderson, Chris Holzer, Kate Irwin, Susan Johnston, John Jones, Jane Kendall, Janet Laughlin, Karen Loccisano, Bob Marstall, Michelle Noiset, Tom Noonan, Beverly Pardee, Diane Patterson, Karen Pellaton, Norma Rahn, Gail Roth, Sally Schaedler, Nancy Schill, Blanche Sims, Suzan Swan, Den Schofield, Irene Trivas, George Ulrich, James Watling, Linda Weller, George Wenzel, Lane Yerkes.

Contributing Student Artists: Kerri Allen, Anisha Bhargava, Shane Bornstein, Jaimee Braverman, Wendy Chang, Jack Chekijian, Amy Conway, Heather Frank, Russell Goss, Hiroshi Kenjo, Injune Kim, Tim Liao, Jessica Lim, Jeffrey Mayer, Michael Meikson, Lindsey Melnick, Jonathan Mooallem, Daniel Moon, Rajiv Parikh, June Park, Carolina Pepe, Jaimee Schwartz, Steven Song, Gene Tan, Jaimee Vogel, David Wishnia.

Photographs: All photographs by Silver Burdett & Ginn (SB&G) unless otherwise noted. **Unit 1** 5: Steve Allen/Peter Arnold, Inc. 18: Victoria Beller-Smith for SB&G. 22: *b.* Dan De Wilde for SB&G. 23: Dan De Wilde for SB&G. 24: Victoria Beller-Smith for SB&G. 25: *t.* Victoria Beller-Smith for SB&G; *b.* Michal Heron for SB&G. 28, 29: Victoria Beller-Smith for SB&G. 30: Michal Heron for SB&G. 31: Dan De Wilde for SB&G. **Unit 2** 35: © John Bova/Photo Researchers, Inc. 55: Victoria Beller-Smith for SB&G. **Unit 3** 61: Dan De Wilde for SB&G. 72: Victoria Beller-Smith for SB&G. 73: *l.* © Bill Wakslicht/Leo deWys, Inc; *r.* Frank Oberle/Bruce Coleman. 93: Breck Kent. **Unit 4** 97: Mark Sherman/Bruce Coleman. 109, 115: Victoria Beller-Smith for SB&G. 118, 119, 125: Michal Heron for SB&G. **Unit 5** 133: Simon Trevor/Bruce Coleman. 152, 155: Victoria Beller-Smith for SB&G. 157: L.L.T. Rhodes/Taurus Photos. **Unit 6** 161: L. West/Bruce Coleman. 183: Victoria Beller-Smith for SB&G. 191: E.F. Bernstein/Peter Arnold, Inc. 193, 194: Victoria Beller-Smith for SB&G. 195: Picasso, *Bird in a Tree.* The Justin K. Thannhauser Collection, Solomon R. Guggenheim Foundation, New York. Photo by Carmelo Gnadagno. **Unit 7** 199: © Susan McCartney/Photo Researchers, Inc. 210: Bill Meng, New York Zoological Society. 214: Rodney Jones for SB&G. 219: E.R. Degginger. **Unit 8** 223: Rodney Jones for SB&G. 236—241: Victoria Beller-Smith for SB&G.

Contributing Writers: Anne Maley; Ann Poole; Julie Small; Rebecca Wade

Acknowledgments continued on page 250

CONNOLLY BRANCH

Dear Boys and Girls,

   We hope you will like this English book.
It can help you be a better thinker, reader,
writer, speaker, and listener.

You as a Learner

   How do you get ideas for what you want to write?
Look at pages 24 and 25. You will find out about
the Writing Process.

11 The Writing Process

1. Prewriting

   Prewriting is getting ideas for your writing.
It is finding as many ideas as you can. It
is discovering an idea that you want to
write about.

Now look at page 160.

A Special Invitation to Books

Emma
by Wendy Kesselman

Emma gets a painting for her birthday. It shows the village where she grew up. Emma remembers her village differently, so she buys her own paints and becomes an artist.

Look Again
by Tana Hoban

You will want to look closely at the photographs in this book. You see only a part of a picture on each page. You guess what the picture is. Then you can lift the page to see if you are right.

Guess What
by Beau Gardner

This book plays a guessing game with you. First you see part of an animal. You guess what the animal is. Then you turn the page for the answer.

Use Your Head, Dear
by Aliki

Charles is an alligator who cannot remember anything. He gets things mixed up. He forgets what he is doing. Then his father gives him a perfect present.

How to Find a GOOD Book
Read the book jacket before you choose a book. The jacket cover will tell you what the book is about.

There are eight pages like this in your book. They are at the beginning of each unit. You will find out about books you may want to read. You will find hints about how to find other good books to read.

You as a Thinker

How do you remember things? If you look at the lesson that begins on page 172, you will find one way to help you remember.

You as a Reader

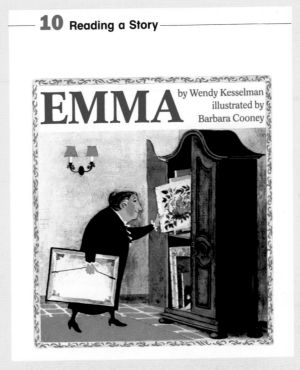

10 Reading a Story

EMMA
by Wendy Kesselman
illustrated by
Barbara Cooney

The story <u>Emma</u> begins on page 174. When you read this story, you will discover what Emma remembered and why it was important to her.

You as a Speaker and Listener

Speaking and listening help you to share ideas, to remember, and to learn. In the lesson on remembering, you will talk with a partner. After you read <u>Emma</u>, you will talk about the story.

You as a Writer

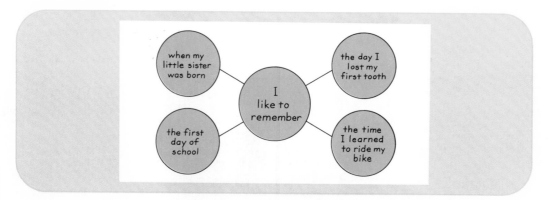

The **Thinking–Reading–Writing** connection comes together in the Writing Project that begins on page 190. You will use what you learn about remembering. You will think about Emma, and then share something that you remember.

We hope you will have a good year in school as you enjoy this book.

Sincerely yours,

Your Authors

Contents

unit 2

unit 4

unit 8

resources

HANDWRITING MODELS

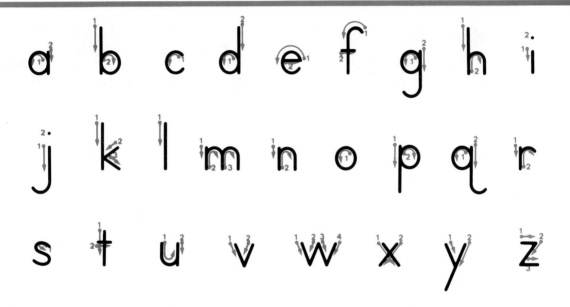

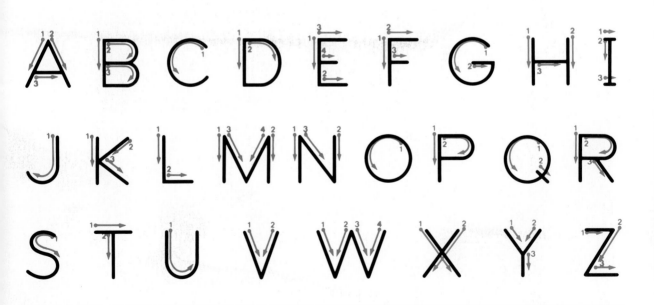

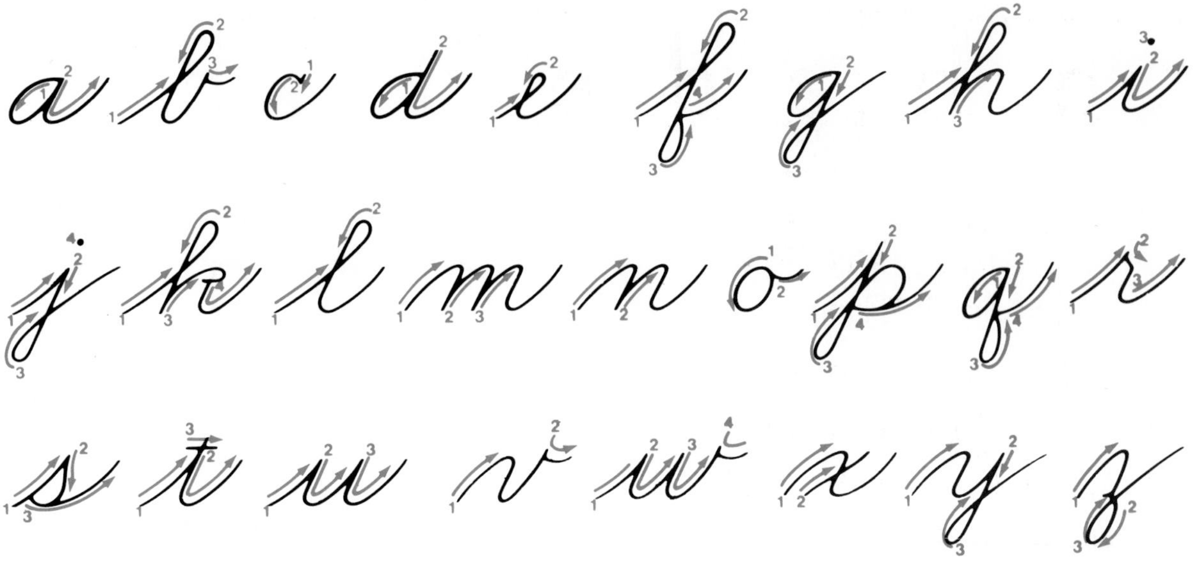

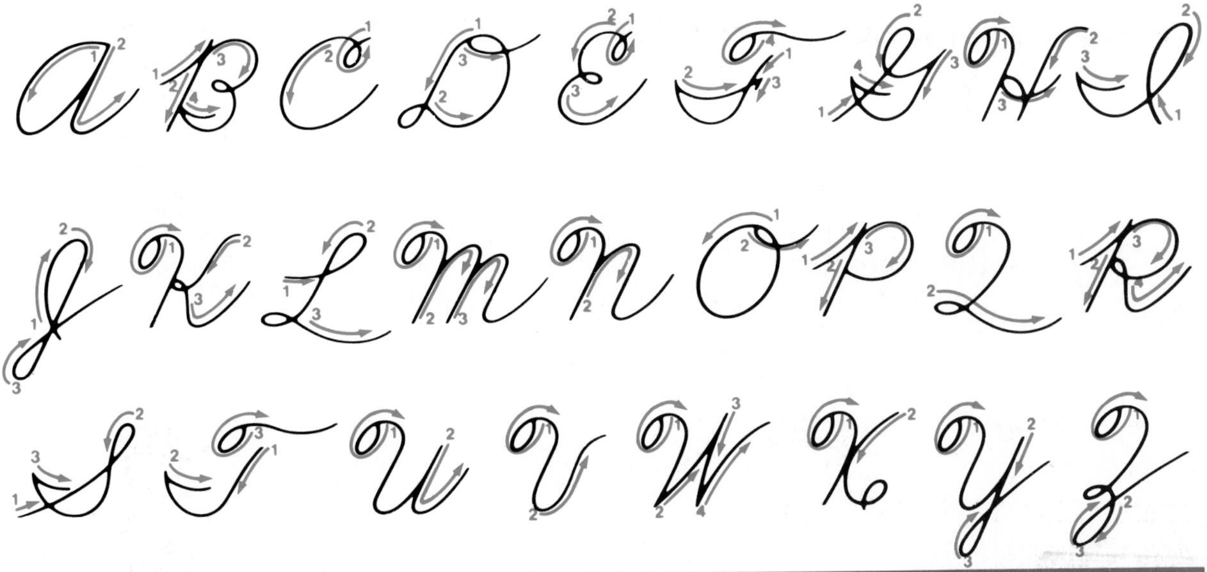

Harriet Reads Signs and More Signs

by Betsy and Giulio Maestro

Harriet reads many signs while she takes a walk. Then she sees one that is her favorite. Which sign do you think it is?

I Read Signs

by Tana Hoban

Signs tell drivers and walkers what to do. This book has many pictures of street signs. See if you know what each sign means.

Signs

by Ron and Nancy Goor

Signs are everywhere. You see signs every day. This book has pictures of many signs. What do they say? What do they mean?

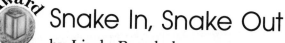

Snake In, Snake Out

by Linda Banchek

In this story a woman gets a pet bird and a pet snake. What do you think happens to them? The direction word on each page will tell you.

How to Find a GOOD Book

Do you have a favorite animal? Look for a book about that animal.

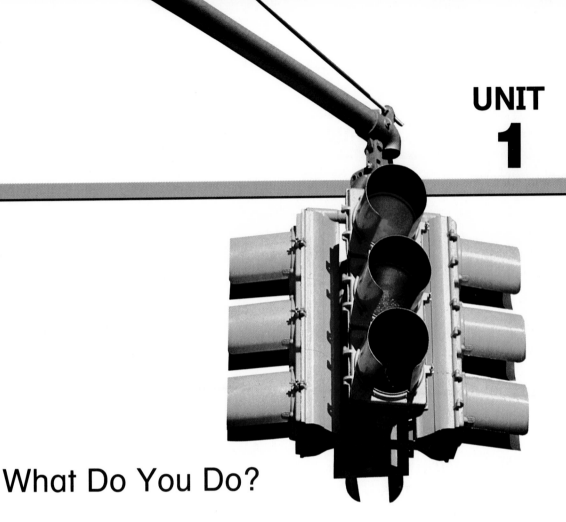

What Do You Do?

Oh, what do you do when the light turns red,
The light turns red, the light turns red?
Oh, what do you do when the light turns red
On the way to school?

You stop and wait when the light turns red,
The light turns red, the light turns red.
You stop and wait when the light turns red
On the way to school.

—Mary Jaye

1 Speaking in Sentences

A **sentence** tells a complete idea.

Jill kicked the ball.

The sentence is about Jill.
It tells what she did.

▶ What else can you say about the picture?
Tell about it in a sentence.

▶ Which picture does each sentence tell about?
Match each sentence with a picture.

1. Jill went over the wall.　**a.**

2. The dog chased the ball.　**b.**

3. The ball is in the mud.　**c.**

Some groups of words are not sentences.
The teams is not a sentence.
It does not tell what the teams do.
The teams run to the field. is a sentence.

The teams
The teams run to the field.

▶ Write the sentence from each pair.

4. a. Our team
b. Our team gets ready.

5. a. The game begins.
b. The game

6. a. Many people
b. Many people watch.

7. a. The small ball
b. The small ball rolls.

8. a. The game ends.
b. The long game

▶ **Apply** What game do you like to play?
Draw a picture and tell about it.

2 Statements

- Begin a sentence with a **capital letter**.
- End a **telling sentence**, or **statement**, with a **period** $\boxed{.}$.

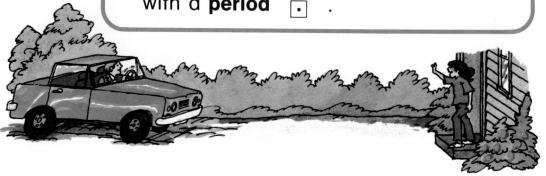

The blue car stops.

▶ Write the correct sentence from each pair.

1. **a.** the car comes
   b. The car comes.

2. **a.** dad gets out
   b. Dad gets out.

3. **a.** He has a box.
   b. he has a box

4. **a.** He gives it to me.
   b. he gives it to me

5. **a.** a frog hops out
   b. A frog hops out.

▶ Write each sentence correctly.

6. the clowns play tricks

7. six clowns ride in a car

8. one clown has a funny hat

9. the clowns run around

10. we laugh at the clowns

▶ **Apply**　What is happening in this picture?
Write three statements about it.
The words in the box can help you.

bike	dog	funny	runs
bird	drum	monkey	trick
circus	flies	plays	wagon
clown		rides	

3 Questions

> - Begin a sentence with a capital letter.
> - End an **asking sentence**, or **question**, with a **question mark** ⟦?⟧ .

Where is my cat**?**

▶ Write the correct question from each pair.

1. **a.** Did it go out?
   b. did it go out

2. **a.** who can find it
   b. Who can find it?

3. **a.** is it lost
   b. Is it lost?

4. **a.** Will it come back?
   b. will it come back

5. **a.** What color is it?
   b. what color is it

6. **a.** did you open this
   b. Did you open this?

7. **a.** Can you come here?
   b. can you come here

8. **a.** is this your cat
   b. Is this your cat?

▶ Copy all the sentences.
Then circle the questions.

9. The cat was in the desk.

10. Did you guess where it was?

11. Do you like guessing games?

12. We played one in school.

13. How many guesses did you have?

14. Can you think of another one?

15. I think I can.

▶ **Apply**   Read what each child asks.
Write each question correctly.

16.   17.   18.

4 Parts of a Sentence

A sentence has two parts.
It has a **naming part** and a **telling part.**

Our class visited a museum.

Our class names who the sentence is about.

visited a museum. tells what our class did.

▶ Match the sentence parts.
Then say the complete sentences.

1. One room	**a.** put bones together.
2. Museum workers	**b.** still grow today.
3. Some dinosaurs	**c.** had dinosaur models.
4. Some of the plants	**d.** ate plants.

► Match the sentence parts.
Then write the complete sentences.
The picture can help you.

5. The museum trip   **e.** likes her dinosaur model.

6. All of us   **f.** was fun.

7. Lisa   **g.** takes a picture of it.

8. Jim   **h.** want to go again.

► **Apply**   Copy the sentences.
Circle each naming part.
Put a line under each telling part.

9. We went on a bus.

10. The ride was short.

11. Our class likes trips.

12. Some reports are finished.

13. The pictures will be ready soon.

14. Our teacher likes our work.

5 Word Order in Sentences

ride bike to I school. a
I ride a bike to school.

The first group of words is not a sentence.
It is not in an order that makes sense.
I ride a bike to school. is a sentence.

▶ Copy the groups of words that are sentences.

1. **a.** children to Some school. walk
   b. Some children walk to school.

2. **a.** Others ride on a bus.
   b. ride bus. on Others

3. **a.** you How to get school? do
   b. How do you get to school?

4. **a.** skate? anyone Does
   b. Does anyone skate?

▶ Write the words in sentence order.

5. outdoors. go We

6. you slide? Did

7. We races. run

8. Will you soccer? play

9. jump rope. children Some

10. time to it Is go in?

▶ **Apply**   Read the story. Put each group of words in sentence order.

    After lunch we story a good read.
It about was three billy goats a and troll.
The troll bridge off a fell.
Then the crossed goats the bridge.

Sentence Combining

> ● Some sentences can be combined.

Grammar
and Writing
Workshop

A. Captain Kid jumps.
B. Captain Kid flies.
A + B. Captain Kid jumps and flies.

Sentences **A** and **B** have the same naming part.
The telling parts can be put together with **and**.
Another word for put together is **combined.**

Read the sentences below.
Then tell how they can be combined.

1. John **swims**.
   John **dives**.

2. Mike **sang**.
   Mike **danced**.

3. Carmen **ate soup**.
   Carmen **drank milk**.

4. Sandra **rides horses**.
   Sandra **trains dogs**.

C. Bill went to the game.

D. Ann went to the game.

C + D. Bill and Ann went to the game.

Sentences **C** and **D** have the same telling part. The naming parts can be combined with **and**.

Tell how the sentences below can be combined.

5. **Boys** go to school.
   Girls go to school.

6. **Kittens** are cute.
   Baby ducks are cute.

Use **and** to combine the words in dark type.
Write the new sentence.

7. I **run**.
   I **win**.

9. Birds **build nests**.
   Birds **lay eggs**.

8. **Sue** went to the fair.
   Jim went to the fair.

10. **My sister** can read.
    I can read.

6 Having a Discussion

> **Rules for Having a Discussion**
> 1. Speak clearly.
> 2. Listen to others.
> 3. Take turns.
> 4. Stay on the topic.

A discussion is talking with other people. You can share ideas. You can discuss a problem. You can talk about ways to solve a problem.

▶ Have a class discussion. Talk about ways to make your classroom less noisy. Follow the rules for having a discussion. Your teacher will write down your ideas.

▶ **Apply** Have a class discussion. Talk about books you have read. Follow the rules for having a discussion.

7 Giving Directions

How to Give Directions

1. Speak clearly.
2. Tell what to do one step at a time.
3. Tell each step in the correct order.
4. Use words like **first, next, then,** and **last.**

▶ Tell how to plant a flower.
Use the pictures to help you give directions.

1.

2.

3.

4.

▶ **Apply** Give directions to a classmate.
Tell how to feed a pet.

8 Following Directions

The children in Mr. Samuel's class were going to paint a floor. He gave them these directions.

1. Get a bucket of paint, a paintbrush, and an old shirt.
2. Start in the corner opposite the door.
3. Put the paintbrush in the paint. Brush the paint on the floor.

This is how it looked when they were finished.

▶ Write the direction they did not follow.

▶ What happened to them? Write your answer.

Mrs. Doyle wrote directions for her class.
They were going to make clowns. You can
make one, too. Follow these directions.

1. Get scissors, glue, and paper
of different colors.

2. Cut a large circle for the body and
a small circle for the head.
Glue them together.

3. Cut a triangle for a hat.
Cut some hair. Glue them on.

4. Cut arms, legs, gloves, and shoes.
Glue them on.

5. Cut eyes, a nose, and a mouth.
Glue them on.

6. Add anything else you want.

▶ **Apply**   Listen as a classmate tells
you how to draw a shape picture.
Follow the directions.

9 Talking on the Telephone

How to Make a Telephone Call
1. Dial the number carefully.
2. Say hello and give your name.
3. Tell why you are calling.
4. Be polite.

▶ Work with a partner.
Act out making telephone calls.

1. Call a friend.
   Invite your friend to visit you.

2. Call the library.
   Ask when the story hour is.

3. Call a neighbor.
   Tell the neighbor you will rake leaves.

4. Call someone in your family.
   Thank the person for your birthday gift.

▶ **Apply** Write a list. Give different reasons for making a telephone call.

10 Taking a Message

How to Take a Message

1. Write who the message is for.
2. Write who called.
3. Write what the person said.
4. Sign your name.

Dan tried to call Liz.

    Ruth: Hello.
    Dan: Hello. This is Dan. Is Liz there?
    Ruth: No, this is Ruth. Liz is out.
          Can I help you?
    Dan: Our soccer team will practice
          tomorrow afternoon at 4:00.
    Ruth: Thank you. I'll tell her.

▶ Write the message Ruth should take.
Use a form like the one below.

```
A message for ___   Who called? ___
The message is _____
_____
        This message is from ___
```

▶ **Apply**   Practice making phone calls with a partner.
Write a message on a piece of paper. Use the form
Ruth used.

11 The Writing Process

1. Prewriting

Prewriting is getting ideas for your writing. It is finding as many ideas as you can. It is discovering an idea that you want to write about.

2. Writing

Writing is putting your ideas on paper. Keep writing. You may think of more to say as you write. Do not worry if you make mistakes. You will fix them later.

3. Revising

Revising is changing your writing to make it better. Read your writing aloud. You can ask another person to listen. Together, talk about what you wrote. This will help you decide what to change.

4. Publishing

Publishing is sharing your writing. First you check your writing for mistakes. This is called **proofreading.** Next you make a neat copy. Then you let others enjoy your writing.

12 Writing a Classroom Message

Messages are important. They give information. You read messages in many different places. You and your classmates will write messages for your classroom. You can make signs to share your messages.

Writing Project

1. Prewriting

▶ Messages give different kinds of information. Talk about these classroom messages.

Messages give directions.

Messages say "Hello."

Messages tell how we feel.

Messages ask us to be thoughtful.

▶ What messages should be in your classroom?
What information would be helpful? Name as
many ideas as you can. Your teacher will
make a list of your ideas.

▶ Choose an idea for your classroom message.

2. Writing

▶ Now write a message for your classroom.
Be sure to use sentences.

3. Revising

▶ Ask a classmate to read your message. Talk about what you wrote. Ask questions.

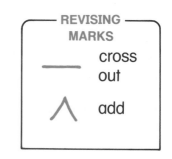

- Will everyone understand my message?

- Do I need to add words?

Look at the message Ross wrote. He wanted to say more, so he added some words.

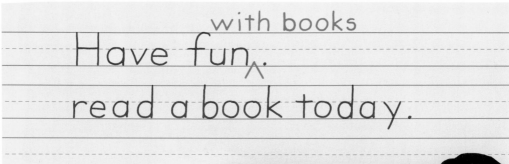

with books
Have fun∧.
read a book today.

▶ Now revise your message. Use the revising marks to make changes.

4. Publishing

▶ Proofread your writing. Use the proofreading marks to make corrections. These questions will help you proofread.

- Did I spell each word correctly?

- Did I begin each sentence with a capital letter?

- Did I use the correct mark at the end of each sentence?

Have fun. ^with books

read a book today.

▶ Make a sign. Copy your message neatly on your sign. Then hang your sign where it belongs in the classroom. Be sure everyone can see it.

A Journal

A journal is a special book to write in. You can write about yourself in your journal. You can write about what is important to you. Write down ideas that you want to save. Later, use your journal to get ideas for your writing.

Write in your journal every day.

1. Write the date at the top of the page.
2. Write about anything you want.
3. You can draw a picture to go with your writing.

Wait—

Social Studies

Schools Now and Then

Schools have changed over the years. Ask a grandparent, an older relative, or a neighbor what school was like for them. What things are different now? What things are the same?

Share what you learned with your class.

Sentences

A. Find the sentences and write them.

1. **a.** My puppy and I
   b. I have a puppy.

3. **a.** Now the bell
   b. The bell rings.

2. **a.** He told a story.
   b. A funny story

4. **a.** The sun is bright.
   b. The sun in the sky

B. Write each sentence correctly.

5. he likes this book

7. she rides a pony

6. my coat is blue

8. the plant needs water

C. Find the questions and write them.

9. **a.** Did you find it?
   b. Matt found a penny.

10. **a.** She will come later.
    b. Will you come with us?

11. **a.** Can you see me?
    b. We see two boys.

12. **a.** A rabbit hopped by.
    b. Do you like rabbits?

D. Copy the sentences. Circle the naming part. Put a line under the telling part.

13. Lenny has a cat.

15. The ice is smooth.

14. We saw a train.

16. I need a new pencil.

E. Write the words in sentence order.

17. home Meg yet? Is

19. deer. Ed a saw

18. game fun. This is

20. is Who boy? that

Telephone

F. Ted called Ron. Ted wanted Ron to meet him at the zoo. Kim answered the phone. Write each part of the message Kim should take.

A message for __21__   Who called? __22__

The message is __23__

This message is from __24__

A Special Invitation to Books

Q Is for Duck
by Mary Etting and
Michael Folsom
This is a special kind of
alphabet book. The letters
stand for funny things. The
book says Q is for Duck.
Can you guess why?

A Hole Is to Dig
by Ruth Krauss
Do you know what a
mountain is for? Do you
know what mashed
potatoes are for? This tiny
book will tell you these
things and more.

All Butterflies
by Marcia Brown
Do you like butterflies? If
you do, you will like the
pictures in this book. They
are all woodcuts of
beautiful butterflies.

Anno's Alphabet
by Mitsumasa Anno
This alphabet book has a
large picture of an object to
go with each letter. Can
you name all the objects?

How to Find a GOOD Book
Ask your librarian for a book your family can read
aloud together.

Open House

If I were a tree
I'd want to see
a bird with a song
on a branch of me.

And down by my roots
I'd want a mouse
With six little mouselings
in her house.

—*Aileen Fisher*

1 Nouns for People and Places

> ● A **noun** names a person, place, or thing.

My father flies jets to many cities.

The words **father**, **jets**, and **cities** are nouns.
The noun **father** names a person.

▶ Find a noun for a person in each sentence.
Then write the nouns.

1. Here comes the pilot.

2. A girl flew on a jet.

3. Her brother went, too.

4. One man fell asleep.

5. Many friends were waiting.

▶ The nouns in the box name places.
Find the nouns that belong in the sentences.
Then write the sentences.

lake farm airport home store city

6. We went to the ___ to see jets landing.

7. We rode past a ___ on our way.

8. Then we saw tall buildings in the ___ .

9. People were buying food in the ___ .

10. Other people were in boats on the ___ .

11. We ate dinner at ___ .

▶ **Apply**   Copy the sentences. Circle the nouns that name people. Put a line under the nouns that name places.

12. My sister went to the park.

13. Your mother is in the bank.

14. That cook works at the airport.

15. My friend moved to another town.

16. The painter is painting the barn.

2 Nouns for Things

This poem has eight nouns that name things.
There is a line under the first one.

Susan peeked into her <u>closet.</u>
She saw —
    a kite, a bat,
    a boat, a hat,
    a wheel, a shoe,
    and a monkey or two.

▶ **1-8.** Write the eight nouns.

▶ Copy the sentences below.
Circle the nouns.

  9. My balloon flies high.

10. Where is the kitten?

11. I ride my bicycle.

12. Do you like the game?

13. A football is hard to catch.

14. Who has the box?

▶ **Apply**   What else could be in the closet?
Write a list of things you might find.

3 One or More than One

> ● Many words add **-s** to mean **more than one**.

toy + s = toys

▶ Add **-s** to the words.
Then write them in the correct sentences.

> track friend train
> tree car

My two __a__ and I
love toy __b__ . Today
we put a gate by the __c__ .
When it went down, a bus
and two __d__ had to stop. We
made some __e__ and bushes.

4 Other Words for More than One

mouse

mice

These are other words for one and more than one.

One	More than One
foot	feet
tooth	teeth
goose	geese
mouse	mice

One	More than One
man	men
woman	women
child	children

▶ Think about the words in the charts. Then complete the sentences.

1. I lost two ＿＿.

2. Three ＿＿ didn't lose any.

3. Do ＿＿ have teeth?

4. I know ＿＿ do.

5. Some ＿＿ and ＿＿ are dentists.

5 Compounds

> A word made from two words is a **compound**.

class + room = classroom

▶ **1–2.** Write two compounds from the poem.

I wore a newspaper raincoat,
I wore a newspaper hat,
and my feet
went splattering down the street
as fast as the rain could spat.

—Aileen Fisher

▶ Put the words together. Write the compounds.

3. rain	**a.** plane	**6.** space	**d.** ball
4. air	**b.** flake	**7.** sail	**e.** ship
5. snow	**c.** bow	**8.** base	**f.** boat

▶ Find a compound for each sentence.
Then write the sentences.

9. We have a good ___ team.
10. Our ___ is on the lake today.

6 Synonyms

- **Synonyms** are words that have almost the same meaning.

This **road** goes to the lake.
This **street** goes to the lake.

The words **road** and **street** are synonyms.
They mean almost the same thing.

▶ Write each sentence below.
Use these words as synonyms for the words
in dark type.

kind   woods   save

1. Our picnic is in the **forest**.

2. Please **keep** these papers.

3. You are a **nice** friend.

▶ Write these words in the story.
Use one for each word in ( ).

began   happy   fluffy   hide
put   little   looking   hole

Once there was a (small) __a__
puppy. His fur was (soft) __b__ .
He wanted to (bury) __c__ his toy.
Was anyone (peeking) __d__ ? The
puppy (started) __e__ to dig. Soon
there was a big (opening) __f__ in
the ground. He (placed) __g__ his toy
in and covered it up. Now he was (glad) __h__ .

Writing with Nouns

> ● Use exact nouns to make your writing better.

A. The animal jumps.
B. The horse jumps.

Both sentences above tell that something jumps. Sentence B tells more. It tells what kind of animal jumps. **Horse** is a more exact noun than **animal**. When you write, use exact nouns. Then the reader will know what you really mean.

The Noun Game   Read the nouns below. Think of a more exact noun for each one. Draw a picture of your exact noun.

1. a place
2. a food
3. clothing

4. a sport
5. a toy
6. an animal

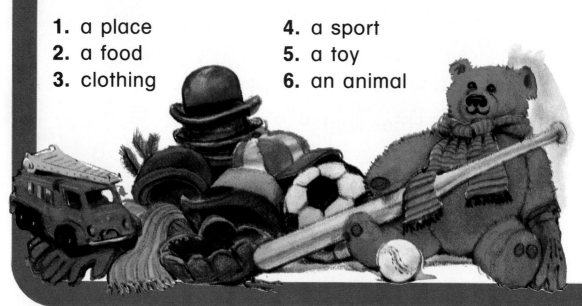

The Noun Switch Write a more exact noun for each underlined noun. Use the words in the Noun Bank.

> **Noun Bank**
>
> chicken   milk   dinner   corn   circle
> birdhouse   peach   kitchen   saw   robins

7. We eat in the <u>room</u>.
8. I really like my <u>meal</u>.
9. The <u>vegetable</u> tastes sweet.
10. Tonight we have <u>meat</u>.
11. I will eat a <u>fruit</u>.
12. Last I have some <u>drink</u>.

Write each sentence below. Use exact nouns from the Noun Bank for the underlined nouns.

13. The <u>birds</u> need a home.
14. I built a <u>building</u>.
15. I cut a <u>shape</u> with a <u>tool</u>.

7 ABC Order

Letters of the alphabet are in **ABC order**.
Many lists of words are in ABC order.
A dictionary and a telephone book list words this way.
This order helps when you look for a word or a name.

Alma	555-2130
Bruce	555-2130
Carol	555-1747

▶ Practice ABC order. Write each group of letters.
Then write the missing letters.

ABCDEFGHIJKLMNOPQRSTUVWXYZ

a b c d e f g h i j k l m n o p q r s t u v w x y z

1. b c ___   **4.** u ___ w   **7.** J ___ L   **10.** ___ G H
2. m ___ o   **5.** ___ f g   **8.** ___ S T   **11.** D ___ F
3. ___ i j   **6.** o p ___   **9.** V W ___   **12.** S T ___

▶ Write the letter that comes first in ABC order.

13. g h f   **16.** p i n   **19.** P O Q   **22.** S M V
14. w u v   **17.** l g r   **20.** L J K   **23.** F N J
15. o w t   **18.** x p s   **21.** P H L   **24.** G I D

Look at the first letter of each word.
Use the first letter to write the words
in ABC order.

25. call
ask
bus

26. way
yet
under

27. grass
tree
flower

28. Nan
Luis
Bill
Rosa

29. quick
sail
row

30. house
shine
clean

31. monkey
elephant
tiger

32. eat
get
find
duck

33. ice
hill
jump

34. milk
butter
eggs

35. year
day
week

36. Sara
Don
Frank
Ann

▶ **Apply** Put the words in ABC order.
They will be a sentence.

37. cat a hid black

38. fish does swim every

8 Finding Words in a Dictionary

The words in a dictionary are in ABC order. A dictionary has **entry words**. An entry word is in dark type. The dictionary gives a meaning for each entry word. Some entry words have more than one meaning.

Two **guide words** are at the top of each page. The first guide word is the first entry word. The second guide word is the last entry word on the page.

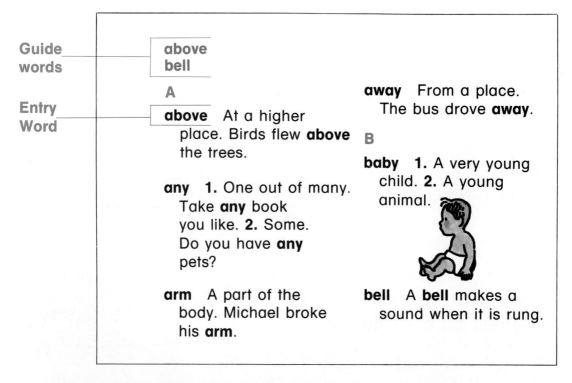

Guide words

above
bell

Entry Word

A

above At a higher place. Birds flew **above** the trees.

any **1.** One out of many. Take **any** book you like. **2.** Some. Do you have **any** pets?

arm A part of the body. Michael broke his **arm**.

away From a place. The bus drove **away**.

B

baby **1.** A very young child. **2.** A young animal.

bell A **bell** makes a sound when it is rung.

▶ Look at the entry for **baby**. Write the number of the meaning that goes with each sentence below.

1. The bird fed its **baby**.

2. The **baby** has a teddy bear.

► Put the words in ABC order. If the first letters are the same, look at the second letter.

3. book
   beet
   bird

4. show
   tool
   see

5. feed
   for
   farm

6. long
   letter
   into

7. our
   owl
   one

8. train
   to
   two

► Look at each pair of guide words. Find an entry word in the box that will be on the same page.

near	come	meet
dog	stove	play

9. day
   drop

10. car
    cub

11. party
    purple

12. many
    moon

13. snow
    sway

14. mud
    now

9 Finding Better Words

A Word Finder begins on page 263 in this book. It lists words together that are synonyms. The entries are in ABC order.

▶ Read the entry below for **little**.

little	not of great size. Tom's balloon was <u>little</u>.
quiet	hard to hear. Kevin sang in a <u>quiet</u> voice.
short	not very tall. My baby brother is too <u>short</u> to reach the shelf.
tiny	very, very small. The <u>tiny</u> bug sat on my finger.
young	not having many years. A <u>young</u> cat is a kitten.

Kate asked a question in a little voice.
Kate asked a question in a quiet voice.
The word **quiet** is a better word to describe a voice.

▶ Write a better word for **little** in each sentence below.

1. Pieces of dust are **little**.
2. She is too **little** to go to high school.
3. He is too **little** to reach the swing.

► Read the story.

   Today we are going to the sports shop. Mom promised to **get** me a new baseball glove. I will use it when I play catcher. My new glove will help me **get** the ball. If we beat the Bears, we will **get** a trophy.

► Look up **get** in the Word Finder that begins on page 263. Write a better word for **get** for each blank in the story.

   Today we are going to the sports shop. Mom

promised to __a__ me a new baseball glove. I will

use it when I play catcher. My new glove will help

me __b__ the ball. If we beat the Bears, we will

__c__ a trophy.

► **Apply**   Write a sentence with the word **bad.**
Now find **bad** in the Word Finder. Write your
sentence again. Use a better word for **bad.**

10 Writing an ABC Book

READ WRITE THINK

Writing Project

You and your classmates can make an ABC book. You can share your ABC book with other classes.

1. Prewriting

▶ Name letters of the alphabet. Name a kind of animal that begins with each letter. Your teacher will list your animal alphabet on the chalkboard.

▶ Think of your favorite animal. You can choose one from the class list. You can choose one of your own. Draw a picture of your favorite animal.

2. Writing

▶ Read the sentences in the Animal Alphabet Box.

Animal Alphabet Box

A is for alligator.
G is for giraffe and goat.
K is for kangaroo.
L is for lion and lamb.
P is for panda bear.

▶ Write your own sentence like the ones in the box. Then write more information about your animal. Do any of the words in the Word Bank describe your animal?

Word Bank

gentle	ugly
bold	fierce
beautiful	wild
tame	huge
noisy	lovable

3. Revising

▶ Read your sentences to a classmate. Talk about your writing. These questions will help you.

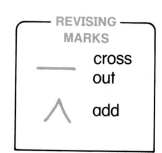

REVISING MARKS

—— cross out

∧ add

• Did I say what I wanted to?

• Does each sentence tell a complete idea?

Look at Jody's sentences. She added a word to tell a complete idea. She also changed a word.

P is for panda bear.

A panda is black and white.

It has sircles around its

eyes. They look like glasses.

A panda is cuddly. I

would love to hold one.
hug

▶ Now revise your writing. Use the revising marks to make changes.

4. Publishing

▶ Proofread your writing. Use the proofreading marks to make corrections. These questions will help you proofread.

- Did I spell each word correctly?

- Did I begin each sentence with a capital letter?

- Did I use the correct mark at the end of each sentence?

It has ~~sircles~~ *circles* around its eyes. *They* look like glasses.

▶ Copy your sentences neatly. Then make a class book. Put all the pages together in ABC order. Be sure to put your pictures in, too. Share your ABC book with other classes.

A Naming Game

You can make a Naming Game. Make a game board that looks like this. Write the name of one group in each square.

Make a set of alphabet cards. Make one card for each letter of the alphabet. Get two buttons.

names of foods	Kinds of animals
first names	places to go
things that are outdoors	things in a home

Play with a partner.

1. Have your partner choose a group on the game board. Put your button on that square.
2. Draw a letter card.
3. Name a word. The word must begin with the letter on your card. The word must belong to the group your partner chose.
4. Take turns playing with your partner.
5. Make a list of words you name for each group.

Social Studies

A code is made up of symbols that stand for letters. Codes have been used for hundreds of years to send messages. Some were secret messages. Messages were sent by telegraph in Morse code.

A	B	C	D	E	F	G	H	I
•—	—•••	—•—•	—••	•	••—•	——•	••••	••

J	K	L	M	N	O	P	Q	R
•———	—•—	•—••	——	—•	———	•——•	——•—	•—•

S	T	U	V	W	X	Y	Z
•••	—	••—	•••—	•——	—••—	—•——	——••

Apply   Break the code. What does this say?

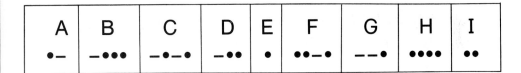

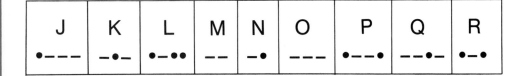

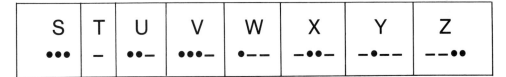

Checkpoint: Unit 2

Nouns

A. Write the noun in each sentence.

1. The store is closed. **3.** My uncle is tall.
2. Is that cat asleep? **4.** Where is my coat?

B. Write the word that means more than one.

5. tooth teeth   **8.** mouse mice
6. balls ball   **9.** desks desk
7. hats hat   **10.** game games

C. Put the words together. Write the compounds.

11. sun   **a.** boat   **14.** scare **d.** cup
12. sail **b.** room   **15.** snow   **e.** storm
13. class **c.** light   **16.** tea   **f.** crow

Synonyms

D. Write the synonym for each word in dark type.

17. Jeff picked a **large** pumpkin. big   thin
18. I feel **happy** today.   sleepy   glad
19. Please wash the **dish**.   spoon   plate
20. We ran into the **woods**.   forest   lake

ABC Order

E. Write the entry word that goes with each set of guide words.

21. **had**
hill   **help**   **hop**   **hurry**

22. **scarf**
sheep   **slide**   **send**   **safe**

Word Finder

F. Read the entry word for **bright**. Then write a better word for **bright** for each sentence.

bright	full of light. The stars are <u>bright</u> tonight.
cheerful	happy or gay. We sang a <u>cheerful</u> song.
clever	smart or skillful. Ben has a <u>clever</u> idea.

23. Tina showed us a **bright** trick.

24. Joe has a **bright** smile.

A Special Invitation to Books

 ## Rosie's Walk
by Pat Hutchins

Rosie, the hen, goes for a walk. She walks around the farm. A fox is following her. It looks like he might catch her!

 ## The Lion and the Rat
by La Fontaine

A lion is kind to a rat. One day the rat gets a chance to thank the lion. Only the rat can save the lion's life. How do you think he does it?

 ## Carrot Seed
by Ruth Krauss

A little boy plants a carrot seed. Everyone says it will not grow. The boy waters the seed and pulls up the weeds. Do you think the seed will grow?

 ## The Snowy Day
by Ezra Jack Keats

Peter wakes up and sees snow out his window. He puts on his snowsuit and goes out to play. Peter discovers many things on a snowy day.

 ## How to Find a GOOD Book
Look at the books on display in your library or classroom.

Somersaults

It's fun turning somersaults
and bouncing on the bed,
I walk on my hands
and I stand on my head.

I swing like a monkey
and I tumble and I shake,
I stretch and I bend,
but I never never break.

I wiggle like a worm
and I wriggle like an eel,
I hop like a rabbit
and I flop like a seal.

I leap like a frog
and I jump like a flea,
there must be rubber
inside of me.

—*Jack Prelutsky*

1 What Is a Verb?

- A word that shows action is a **verb**.

We run with the football.

The word **run** is a verb.
It shows something we can do.

▶ Find the verbs in these sentences.
Then write them.

1. We kick soccer balls on the field.

2. I throw a basketball into the hoop.

3. Sandy and John hit baseballs.

4. They jog a mile every day.

5. We bounce balls in the gym.

6. Liz and Allen swim 50 laps a week.

► Write the verbs for the sentences.

dance   write   play   take

act   build   sing   collect

Some people have special things they like to do. Joan and I __a__ things with wood. Margie and Joe __b__ in plays. Ken and Lisa __c__ beautiful pictures with their cameras. Jean, Mike, and Larry __d__ the piano. Betty, Lisa, and Don __e__ songs in a chorus. Doug and Jan __f__ in their tap class. Some people __g__ poems. My sisters __h__ baseball cards.

2 Adding -s to Verbs

> ● Add **-s** to a verb to tell about one person or thing.

One pumpkin grows.   **Two pumpkins grow.**

▶ Write the correct verb for each sentence.

1. A pumpkin (grow, grows) ___ on a vine.

2. At first pumpkins (look, looks) ___ green.

3. A ripe one (look, looks) ___ orange.

4. Mike (pick, picks) ___ a ripe one.

5. Kim and Sue (pick, picks) ___ some, too.

6. The children (make, makes) ___ jack-o'-lanterns.

7. Mike (make, makes) ___ his look funny.

3 Adding *-ed* to Verbs

> ● Many verbs that tell about the past end with **-ed**.

When company came
we peeked in the door
(Rebecca and I)
and squeaked on the floor,
then whispered and ran,
and peeked in once more.

—Aileen Fisher

peek + ed = peeked

▶ **1–4.** Copy the poem.
Put a line under four verbs
that end with **-ed**.

▶ Add **-ed** to the words in ( ).

5. Jan (open) ___ the door.

6. Our company (walk) ___ in.

7. It (rain) ___ all day.

8. We (cook) ___ dinner.

9. Everyone (enjoy) ___ it.

4 Adding -s and -ed to Verbs

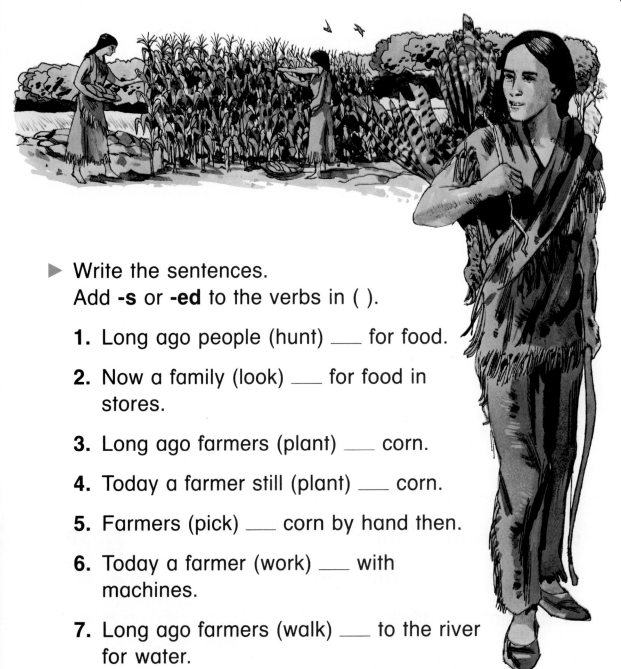

▶ Write the sentences.
Add **-s** or **-ed** to the verbs in ( ).

1. Long ago people (hunt) ___ for food.

2. Now a family (look) ___ for food in stores.

3. Long ago farmers (plant) ___ corn.

4. Today a farmer still (plant) ___ corn.

5. Farmers (pick) ___ corn by hand then.

6. Today a farmer (work) ___ with machines.

7. Long ago farmers (walk) ___ to the river for water.

8. Now water (flow) ___ through pipes to us.

5 The Prefixes *re-* and *un-*

> ● A **prefix** is a letter or letters added to the beginning of a word.

Prefix	Meaning	Examples				
re-	again	re	+	fill	=	refill
un-	not	un	+	hurt	=	unhurt

broken   **un**broken

▶ Write the words that have prefixes.

1. Let's rewrap the gift.
2. Is your shoe untied?
3. They were unhappy.
4. I will rewrite my story.
5. Did you unpack yet?
6. Please renew my book.
7. I relit the fire.
8. She is never unkind.

▶ Rewrite the sentences.
Add the prefix in ( ) to the word in dark type.

9. (un-) The door is **locked**.

10. (re-) Please **play** the song.

6 Opposites

The train stops.   **The train starts.**

The words **stops** and **starts** are **opposites**.
They have opposite meanings.

▶ Match the opposites.

1. laugh	**a.** sit	**4.** tall	**d.** dry
2. stand	**b.** open	**5.** on	**e.** short
3. close	**c.** cry	**6.** wet	**f.** off

▶ Find the opposites for the words in dark type.

Write them in the sentences.

7. The train doors **close**.

8. We **stand** in the first car.

9. We get **on** in New City.

► Find the opposites for the words in dark type.
Write them in the sentences.

> young   good-by   land
> cool   late   happy
> outside   shout   long

10. Many jets **take off**.

11. Some trips are **short**.

12. I see **old** people.

13. Sometimes they **whisper**.

14. People work **inside**.

15. Friends say **hello**.

16. The plane is **early.**

17. Are you **sad?**

18. It is **warm** today.

► **Apply**   Think of a pair of opposites.
Draw a picture to go with each word.
Write a sentence that tells about each
word.

Writing with Verbs

- Use exact verbs to make your writing better.

A. "Stop!" she said.
B. "Stop!" she yelled.

Both sentences above tell what the girl said. Sentence B tells more. It tells how the girl spoke. **Yelled** is a more exact verb than **said.**

The Verb Game Find the exact verbs that are hidden in the puzzle. Then write two of them for each verb listed.

1. go

2. say

3. get

4. look

5. break

c	r	a	c	k	s	u	m
a	s	h	o	u	t	b	a
l	k	w	i	n	a	u	r
l	i	t	e	a	r	y	c
u	p	e	e	k	e	z	h

The Verb Switch   Write a more exact verb
for each underlined verb. Use the words
in the Verb Bank.

```
                    Verb Bank
   bought      cut       kicked      jumped
```

6. She <u>moved</u> the ball away.
7. I <u>got</u> a hat at the store.
8. Bill <u>hurt</u> his finger.
9. Judy <u>went</u> into the pool.

Using the Word Finder   Read the paragraph.
Then look up **cook** in the Word Finder that
begins on page 263. If you find a better word
for **cook**, write it. If you do not find one that
is better, write **cook**.

　　　Dad loves to (**10.** cook) ___. He loves to
(**11.** cook) ___ bacon and eggs. At night he
may (**12.** cook) ___ carrots in a pot. He can
(**13.** cook) ___ rolls in the oven. Most of
all, he likes to (**14.** cook) ___ hamburgers
outside.

7 Discovering

Thinking Skills

Discovering is a way to learn. It is a way to find out new things. You can learn and discover new things. Questions can help you.

▶ With a partner, discover answers to these questions.

1. What sounds can you make with paper?
2. What shapes can you make with paper?
3. How many elephants can you draw on one sheet of paper?

Now, discover something new about your partner. Find answers to questions.

▶ Ask your partner these questions.
Listen carefully to the answers.

1. What are your favorite flying things?
2. What funny things make you laugh?
3. What is the best thing you ever did?

▶ Did you discover something new about your partner? Tell about one new thing you learned.

You as a Thinker

• How do you discover new things?
Tell one way of discovering.

• When do you need to ask questions?
Tell about a time when it is important to ask questions.

EZRA JACK KEATS

THE SNOWY DAY

One winter morning Peter woke up and looked out
the window. Snow had fallen during the night.
It covered everything as far as he could see.

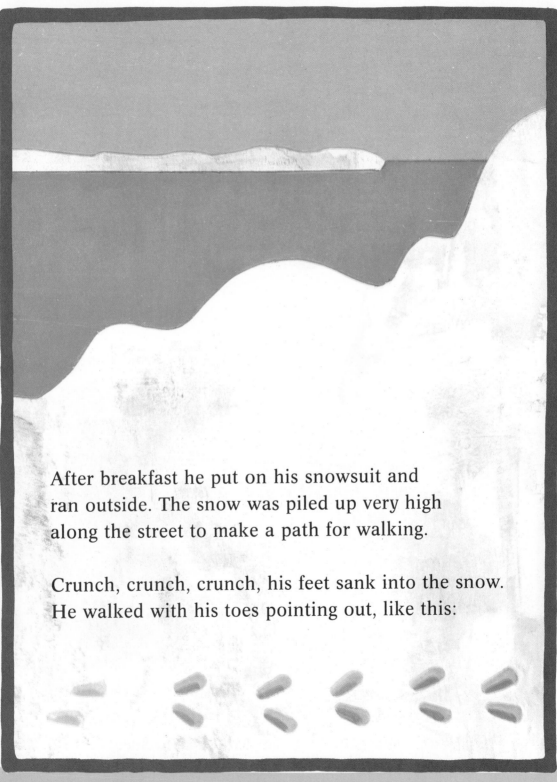

After breakfast he put on his snowsuit and
ran outside. The snow was piled up very high
along the street to make a path for walking.

Crunch, crunch, crunch, his feet sank into the snow.
He walked with his toes pointing out, like this:

He walked with his toes
pointing in, like that:

Then he dragged his feet s-l-o-w-l-y
to make tracks. And he found something
sticking out of the snow that made a new
track. It was a stick—a stick that was just
right for smacking a snow-covered tree.

Down fell the snow—
plop!
—on top of Peter's head.

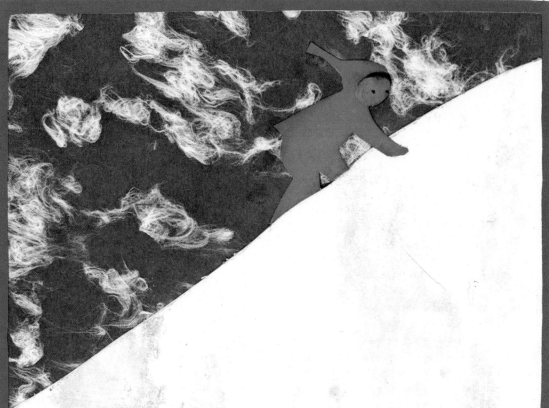

He thought it would be fun to join the big boys in
their snowball fight, but he knew he wasn't old
enough—not yet.

So he made a smiling snowman,
and he made angels.
He pretended
he was a mountain-climber.
He climbed up
a great big tall
heaping mountain of snow—
and slid all the way down.

He picked up a handful of snow—
and another, and still another.
He packed it round and firm
and put the snowball in his pocket
for tomorrow. Then he went into
his warm house.

He told his mother
all about his adventures
while she took off his
wet socks.

And he thought and
thought and thought
about them.

Before he got into bed he looked in his pocket.
His pocket was empty. The snowball wasn't there.
He felt very sad.

While he slept,
he dreamed that
the sun had melted
all the snow away.

But when he woke up
his dream was gone. The
snow was still everywhere.
New snow was falling!

After breakfast he called to his
friend from across the hall, and
they went out together into the
deep, deep snow.

Talking About the Story

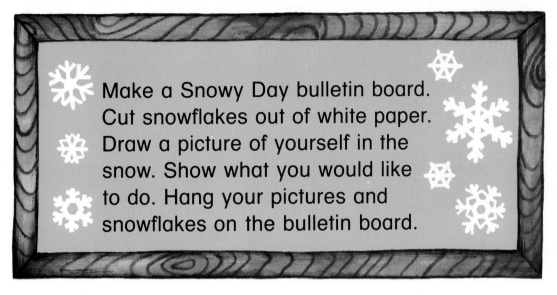

Make a Snowy Day bulletin board. Cut snowflakes out of white paper. Draw a picture of yourself in the snow. Show what you would like to do. Hang your pictures and snowflakes on the bulletin board.

You as a Reader

1. What part of Peter's day did you like best? Tell your classmates about it.

2. Discover new things in a place you already know. Walk around your classroom. Look at things. Touch things. Smell things. Ask questions. Then make a class list. Write the things you discovered.

3. Look at the story. Find verbs that tell what Peter did on a snowy day. Act out the things he did.

You as a Writer

Think about a snowy day. What exciting thing could happen? Tell what you would write a story about.

9 Telling a Story in Order

▶ Read the sentences about <u>The Snowy Day</u>.
Write the sentences in story order.

Peter put on his snowsuit and went outside.

Peter dreamed that all the snow had melted.

Peter and his friend went outside in the snow.

Peter walked, climbed, and slid in the snow.

▶ Tell the story of <u>The Snowy Day</u> in your own words.

▶ **Apply** Tell your favorite story to the class.
Use story order to tell what happened.

10 Ending a Story

A story needs a good ending. The ending tells what happened. It gives answers to questions the reader has.

▶ Write an ending for the story below. It can be anything you think it should be.

Rosie's dog loved to catch things. Monty could jump and catch things in the air. He could flip over and catch them. He was the best catcher on the block.

The town Rosie lived in was having a special contest just for dogs. On the day of the contest, Rosie and Monty walked to the park. Many dogs were there. Rosie and Monty had to wait in a long line. It was a hot day. They waited a long time.

Finally, a man waved to Rosie. It was Monty's turn. But Monty was asleep.

▶ **Apply**   Draw a comic strip with only two pictures. Your pictures should begin a story. Ask a partner to draw the last picture to finish your story.

Characters:

Narrator	Cardinal	Deer
Child	Weasel	Bear
Chipmunk	Fox	Fly

Setting: A snowy winter day
in the woods

Narrator: One cold winter day, a child was out in the woods. The child was collecting firewood for the family. (Child enters.) While the child was putting sticks on a sled, a mitten fell. The child did not know it was gone. Later, a chipmunk found the mitten.

Chipmunk: Look at that! What a lovely place to keep warm. (Steps inside the mitten.) Oh-h-h, it's so soft.

Cardinal: What a funny home you live in, Chipmunk. Is there room for me? (Steps in.)

Weasel: Well, well. You two look very snug and warm. Will you invite your old friend in?

Chipmunk: I would, but there isn't any room.

Weasel: (Steps in.) Why, I fit perfectly.

Fox: I wonder if I could fit, too. Move over, Weasel. (Steps in.) This is nice.

Deer (softly): Excuse me.

All: What?

Deer: Excuse me. I hope it is not too much to ask. But could you be so kind as to let me in just a small corner? I think I am freezing.

Chipmunk: We don't have any small corners. In fact, we don't have any corners. But I suppose you could squeeze in. (Deer steps in.)

Bear: Just what I was looking for. A place to keep warm.

All: Oh, no! Forget it! No room!

Bear: Nonsense! Everyone breathe in. (Steps in.) See? That wasn't so bad.

Fly: Look at all of those animals stuffed into that mitten. I bet they're warm and dry. Say, folks, how about making room for a teensy, weensy fly?

Chipmunk: Why not? What's a little fly? (Fly flies in.)

All: BANG! (The mitten explodes. All of the animals run away.)

Narrator: A few minutes later, the child came back to look for the mitten. (Child enters.) All the child found was a small thread in the snow. (Child picks up thread and looks puzzled.)

▶ **Apply** Take turns acting out the story.

THINK READ WRITE

Writing Project

12 Writing a Story

You have read a story about Peter's snowy day. Now you can write your own snowy day story. You and your classmates can make a book of stories for the library.

1. Prewriting

▶ Look at the picture. Discover the things that could happen on a snowy day. It may be something real.
It may be something make-believe.

▶ What adventure will your story be about?
Draw a picture to show what will happen.

▶ Show your picture to a classmate. Tell what you
see. Tell what will happen in your story.

2. Writing

▶ Write a story about a snowy
day adventure. The words in
the Word Bank may help you.
If you wish, begin your
story with the words below.

Word Bank	
snowflake	magical
blizzard	frosty
crunch	icicle
shiver	sparkle

One snowy day

3. Revising

▶ Read your story to a classmate.
Talk about what you wrote. These
questions will help you revise.

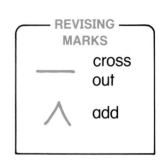

- Did I say enough?

- Did I use exact words?

Here is the beginning of David's story. Look at
the changes he made.

> One snowy day I made
> huge
> a ^ snowball. It rolled away
> from me. It would not stop.
> Then I remembered my raceing
> jumped
> sled. I ~~got~~ on my speedy
> zoomed
> sled and ~~went~~ down the hill.

▶ Now revise your story. Use the revising marks
to make changes. Try to use exact verbs.

4. Publishing

▶ Proofread your story. Use the proofreading marks to make corrections. These questions will help you proofread.

PROOFREADING MARKS

⬭ check spelling

≡ capital letter

- Did I spell each word correctly?

- Did I begin each sentence with a capital letter?

- Did I use the correct mark at the end of each sentence?

Then I remembered my ⟨raceing⟩ *racing*
sled. I ~~got~~ on my speedy *jumped*
sled and ~~went~~ down the hill. *zoomed*

▶ Copy your story neatly. Make a class book of snowy day stories. Be sure to include your pictures. Then put your book in the school library. Everyone will enjoy reading your stories.

Snowy Day Stories
by
Mr. McComb's Class

A Story Puppet

You can make puppets to use for acting out stories.

1. Get an old sock. Put it on your hand.
2. Spread out your hand inside the sock. Close your thumb and fingers around the sock.
3. Glue or paint eyes on it.
4. Glue or paint a mouth on it.
5. Glue or sew on yarn for hair.
6. Add anything else you want.

Science

How a Frog Grows

A baby frog does not look like a grown-up frog. It even has a different name. A baby frog is called a **tadpole**, or **polliwog**.

A tadpole lives in the water. It has a round head and a long tail. The tadpole changes its shape. Soon legs begin to grow.

Last, the tadpole's legs become very long. Its tail gets smaller and disappears. It can hop on the ground. It is not a tadpole any more. It is a frog.

Put the pictures in order.
Write **1** for the young tadpole.
Write **2** for the tadpole growing legs.
Write **3** for the frog.

a.
b.
c.

Verbs

A. Write the verb in each sentence.

1. Rita climbs trees in the yard.
2. The children play hopscotch.
3. Jan and Sue win the races.
4. We walk home from the playground.
5. Scott builds a fort under the oak tree.

B. Write the correct verb in ( ) for each sentence.

6. We (drink, drinks) milk.
7. Karen (get, gets) her boots.
8. Snakes (move, moves) quickly.
9. The ball (roll, rolls) away.

C. Add **-ed** to the verbs in ( ). Write the new words.

10. The dog (bark) a lot.
11. I (jump) over the rope.
12. They (walk) home.
13. We (paint) the fence.

Prefixes

D. Write the words that have prefixes.

14. Beth unfolded her paper.
15. Rick will reread the story.
16. Did Kate reheat the soup?
17. Dan will unwrap the gift.

Opposites

E. Match the opposites.

18. push	**a.** stand	**21.** warm	**d.** large
19. wrong	**b.** right	**22.** small	**e.** low
20. sit	**c.** pull	**23.** high	**f.** cool

Stories

F. Write these sentences in story order.

24. Next we shoveled the snow.
25. It snowed last night.
26. Last we made a snowman.
27. First we got dressed.

A Special Invitation to Books

Blackberry Ink

by Eve Merriam

These funny poems are for reading aloud. Some of the poems are about umbrellas. Some are about breakfast and washing machines. See which poems you like best.

I Met a Man

by John Ciardi

These poems are for fun. You will read silly poems and magical poems in this book. You will even find riddles with the poems.

Go to Bed! A Book of Bedtime Poems

selected by Lee Bennett Hopkins

Do you like to read before you go to bed? These poems are just for that time of night. They tell about teddy bears and stars. They tell about going to bed and dreaming.

A Song I Sang to You

by Myra Cohn Livingston

This poet writes about everyday things. The poems in this book tell about toy boxes and bumping your knee. They tell about tails and whales.

How to Find a GOOD Book

What do you wonder about? Stars? Thunder? Ask for a book about what interests you.

Tugs

Chug! Puff! Chug!
Push, little tug.
Push the great ship here
Close to its pier.

Chug! Puff! Chug!
Pull, strong tug.
Drawing all alone
Three boat-loads of stone.

Busy harbor tugs,
Like round water bugs,
Hurry here and there,
Working everywhere.

— *James S. Tippett*

1 What Is an Adjective?

- An **adjective** tells more about a noun.

I have a puppy.
I have a playful puppy.

The word **puppy** is a noun.
The adjective **playful** tells more about the noun.

▶ Copy the sentences below.
Put a line under the nouns.
Circle the adjectives that tell about the nouns.

1. I wear red boots.
2. We walk in deep snow.
3. He has a long sled.
4. We go down the high hill.
5. She wears soft mittens.
6. I have a warm scarf.
7. We saw big trees.
8. Do you have new skates?
9. This is a sunny day.
10. I like your purple hat.

▶ Find the adjectives to describe the nouns.
Then write them for the sentences.

| best | snowy | hot | round | loud |
| tall | blue | icy | shiny | green |

11. It is a ___ day.

12. We put sand on the ___ sidewalk.

13. Plows make ___ piles of snow.

14. I wear a ___ hat.

15. My ___ friend plays with me.

16. A ___ truck gets stuck.

17. The ___ tire gets flat.

18. We hear a ___ voice.

19. I find a ___ penny.

20. Later we have a ___ drink.

▶ **Apply** Write sentences with adjectives. Tell what winter is like where you live.

2 Words That Tell *How Many*

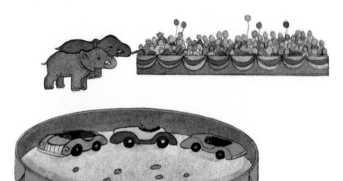

I see two elephants.
There are some cars here.

The words **two** and **some** tell how many.

▶ Copy the sentences below.
Circle the words that tell how many.

1. We see five monkeys on the wire.
2. Each monkey has one umbrella.
3. The elephants eat some peanuts.
4. We buy two bags of popcorn.
5. There are many people here.
6. I see nine clowns in the car.
7. The car has four tires.
8. Did you see some lions?
9. Now ten elephants are in the ring.
10. There are three rings in this circus.

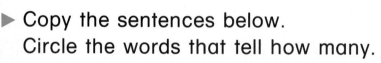

one
two
three
four
five
six
seven
eight
nine
ten

▶ Find the number words that
describe the nouns.
Write them for the sentences.

11. I see ___ clowns riding.
12. Each clown rides on ___ wheel.
13. There are ___ horses in the ring.
14. Then ___ people make a tower.
15. The bottom row has ___ people.
16. A man juggles ___ balls.

▶ **Apply** Draw a circus picture.
Write three sentences about it.
Use number words in your sentences.

3 Words That Tell *What Kind*

red	blue	green	brown
black	yellow	white	orange

▶ Find the color words for the sentences. Then write them for the sentences.

1. A girl wears a ___ jacket.
2. She flies a ___ kite.
3. There is a ___ tail on the kite.
4. A boy walks a ___ dog.
5. He wears a ___ scarf.
6. A ___ car goes by.
7. The car has ___ tires.
8. An ___ cat sits and watches.
9. The ___ tree has a birdhouse.
10. A ___ bird is in the tree.

▶ Words for size and shape help to tell what kind.
Write words from the box for the sentences.

> flat   straight   round   tall
> square   pointed   small   large

11. The food store has a ___ roof.

12. Each other store has a ___ roof.

13. The pet store has a ___ window.

14. The shoe store has a ___ window.

15. A ___ truck is carrying bread.

16. A ___ truck is picking up mail.

17. Cars park in ___ rows.

18. A painter is on a ___ ladder.

4 Words That Compare

- Add **-er** to an adjective to compare two persons, places, or things.
- Add **-est** to an adjective to compare three or more persons, places, or things.

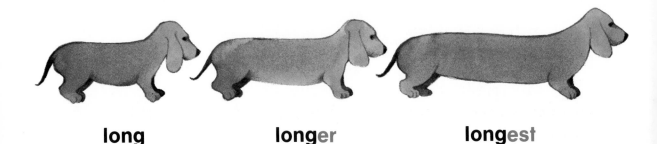

long **longer** **longest**

▶ Add **-er** and **-est** to the words below.

1. tall	**3.** new	**5.** short
2. cold	**4.** low	**6.** soft

▶ Add **-er** to the words in ( ).
Then write them for the sentences.

7. A car is (fast) ___ than a train.
8. A drum is (loud) ___ than a bell.
9. This bag is (light) ___ than that one.
10. The kite is (high) ___ than my house.

▶ Add **-est** to the words in ( ).
Then write them for the sentences.

11. Today is the (short) ___ day in the year.
12. Tonight is the (long) ___ night of all.
13. That is the (tall) ___ building in the world.
14. I wrote the (long) ___ story of all.

▶ Add **-er** or **-est** to the words in ( ).
Then write them for the sentences.

15. A lake is (deep) ___ than a pond.
16. An ocean is the (deep) ___ body of water.
17. I am (old) ___ than my brother.
18. My sister is the (old) ___ child in our family.
19. A turtle is (slow) ___ than a rabbit.
20. A snail is the (slow) ___ of all.

▶ **Apply**   Add **-er** and **-est** to the word **high.**
Write a sentence for each new word.

Writing with Adjectives

● Use adjectives to make your writing more interesting.

A. I saw a house.
B. I saw an old brown house.

Both sentences tell about a house. Sentence B tells more. The words **old** and **brown** tell what the house looked like.

Other adjectives could tell that the house was **tall** and **empty.** When you write, use adjectives to make your writing more interesting.

The Adjective Game   Read the pairs of adjectives and nouns below. They do not belong together. Write the adjective that makes sense for each noun.

round hair	green lips	furry soup
pink grass	salty puppy	curly table

1. ___ hair
2. ___ lips
3. ___ grass

4. ___ soup
5. ___ table
6. ___ puppy

Add-an-Adjective Make the sentences below more interesting. Add an adjective to each one from the Adjective Bank.

> **Adjective Bank**
> muddy silly noisy juicy

7. The ___ storm woke me up.
8. I washed the ___ car.
9. We ate ___ pears.
10. Do you like ___ clowns?

Using the Word Finder Read the paragraph. Then look up **big** in the Word Finder. If you find a better word for **big**, write it. If you do not find one that is better, write **big**.

The (**11.** big) ___ monkey walked into the store. "I'll buy three bananas," he said in a (**12.** big) ___ voice. "I'm a very (**13.** big) ___ monkey at the zoo. Most monkeys only get one banana. I get three!"

5 Finding Patterns

THINK READ WRITE

Thinking Skills

A pattern is something that can be repeated. A pattern can be copied again and again.

▶ Look at each row of shapes. Each row has a pattern. The pattern is repeated three times. Draw each pattern one more time.

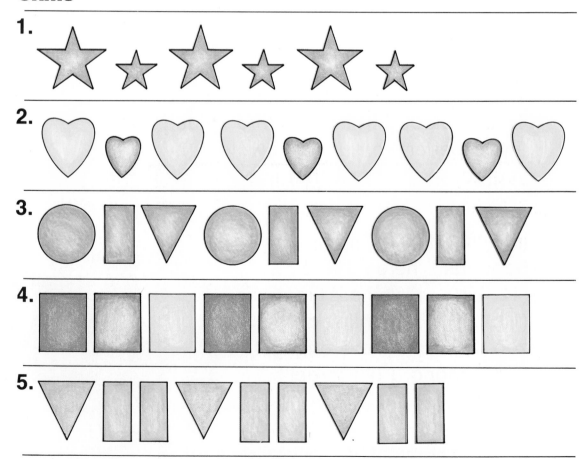

1.

2.

3.

4.

5.

▶ Patterns can be made with sounds. Make these sound patterns.

1. Say the word **louder.** Then clap once. Do this three times.

2. Say the word **chug.** Then very quickly say the words **chug chug.** Do this three times.

3. First say the word **owl.** Then slowly clap twice. Finally, ask the question **Who?** Do this three times.

▶ You can make your own sound pattern. Write a pattern. Use three sounds.

▶ Tell the class your sound pattern. Ask them to repeat your pattern three times.

You as a Thinker

- Have you ever noticed a pattern? Tell about it.

- Tell about a time when you can use a pattern.

6 Reading Poetry

Poets enjoy sharing what they see and hear. In many poems poets tell about themselves. Here are some poems for you to read and enjoy. See how the poets talk about things they like to imagine.

Catch a Little Rhyme

Once upon a time
I caught a little rhyme

I set it on the floor
but it ran right out the door

I chased it on my bicycle
but it melted to an icicle

I scooped it up in my hat
but it turned into a cat

I caught it by the tail
but it stretched into a whale

I followed it in a boat
but it changed into a goat

When I fed it tin and paper
it became a tall skyscraper

Then it grew into a kite
And flew far out of sight...

— Eve Merriam

Skyscraper

Skyscraper, skyscraper,
Scrape me some sky:
Tickle the sun
While the stars go by.

Tickle the stars
While the sun's climbing high,
Then skyscraper, skyscraper,
Scrape me some sky.

— Dennis Lee

Thorn Song

I was walking there along the hill
When a wild rose caught me and held me still.
"You thorns," I said, "don't hold me so:
It's getting dark and I must go."

— Charlotte B. de Forest

Little Snail

I saw a little snail
Come down the garden walk.
He wagged his head this way...that way...
Like a clown in a circus.
He looked from side to side
As though he were from a different country.
I have always said he carries his house
  on his back...
Today in the rain
I saw that it was his umbrella!

— Hilda Conkling

Marisol

My friend's name is Marisol.
Mar is the sea.
Sol is the sun.
I dream, I dream of Marisol.
Sueño del mar,
De mar y sol,
When the golden day is done.

— Charlotte Pomerantz

The Shell

I took away the ocean once,
Spiraled in a shell,
And happily for months and months
I heard it very well.

How is it then that I should hear
What months and months before
Had blown upon me sad and clear,
Down by the grainy shore?

— David McCord

The Bird's Nest

I know a place, in the ivy on a tree,
Where a bird's nest is, and the eggs are three,
And the bird is brown, and the eggs are blue,
And the twigs are old, but the moss is new,
And I go quite near, though I think I should have heard
The sound of me watching, if I had been a bird.

— John Drinkwater

Solitude

I have a house where I go
    When there's too many people,
I have a house where I go
    Where no one can be;
I have a house where I go,
Where nobody ever says "No";
Where no one says anything — so
    There is no one but me.

— A. A. Milne

I Like It When It's Mizzly

I like it when it's mizzly
and just a little drizzly
so everything looks far away
and make-believe and frizzly.

I like it when it's foggy
and sounding very froggy.
I even like it when it rains
on streets and weepy windowpanes
and catkins in the poplar tree
and *me*.

— Aileen Fisher

I'd Like to Be a Lighthouse

I'd like to be a lighthouse
   All scrubbed and painted white.
I'd like to be a lighthouse
   And stay awake all night
To keep my eye on everything
   That sails my patch of sea;
I'd like to be a lighthouse
   With the ships all watching me.

— Rachel Field

Talking About the Poems

Partner reading is one way to enjoy poetry. What is your favorite poem? Draw a picture of your poem. Then take turns, and read your poem to a partner. When your partner reads, listen.

You as a Reader

1. Look for patterns in the poems. When you find one, tell the class what it is.

2. The skyscraper tickles. Thorns catch and hold. Name other objects that do things people do.

3. Aileen Fisher likes drizzly, foggy days. What kind of day do you like? Write adjectives that describe your favorite kind of day.

You as a Writer

Rachel Field liked to imagine that she was a lighthouse. What do you like to imagine? Tell what you would write a poem about.

7 Listening for Rhymes

A poet may create a sound pattern with rhyme. Some poems have pairs of rhyming lines. These lines are called **rhyming couplets.** In a rhyming couplet the last words in the lines rhyme.

▶ Take turns reading the poem aloud.
Listen for the rhyming couplets.

Pick Me Up

Pick me up with a pile of blocks
And carry me past the Cuckoo Clocks!

Pick me up with a pile of hay
And carry me off to Buzzards Bay!

Pick me up with a pile of snow
And carry me out to Idaho!

Pick me up with a pile of twine
And carry me down to the Argentine!

Pick me up with a pile of lava
And carry me over the hills of Java.

Pick me up with a pile of sand
And put me down in Newfoundland.

— William Jay Smith

▶ **1-2.** Look at the poem.
Write two pairs of rhyming words from the poem.

▶ Choose a rhyming couplet from the poem.
Draw a picture to go with the two lines.
Write the rhyming couplet on your picture.
Circle the rhyming words.

▶ **Apply**   Write your own rhyming couplet for the
poem. What would you take with you? Where
would you go?

Pick me up with a ____
And put me down in ____.

8 Acting Out a Poem

▶ Read the poem.

Ayii, ayii, ayii,
My arms, they wave high in the air,
My hands, they flutter behind my back,
They wave above my head
Like the wings of a bird.
Let me move my feet.
Let me dance.
Let me shrug my shoulders.
Let me shake my body.
Let me crouch down.
My arms, let me fold them.
Let me hold my hands under my chin.

— Central Eskimo

▶ Your teacher will divide the class into two groups.
Each group will take turns reading the poem aloud.
The other group will listen and act out the poem.

► The poet tells how the wings of a bird move.
Show how your arms can be the wings of a bird.

► Choose your favorite line from the poem.
Act it out. Ask the class to guess which
line you are acting.

► Apply   Think of all the ways you can move.
Finish these lines with your own words. Then
act them out.

Let me move my ___ .
Let me ___ .

9 Saying a Poem Together

▶ Listen to your teacher read this poem.
Then read the poem with three different groups.

Some One

Group 1: Some one came knocking
At my wee, small door;

Group 2: Some one came knocking,
I'm sure — sure-sure;

Group 3: I listened, I opened,
I looked to left and right,

All: But nought there was a-stirring
In the still dark night;

Group 1: Only the busy beetle
Tap-tapping in the wall,

Group 2: Only from the forest
The screech-owl's call,

Group 3: Only the cricket's whistling
Where the dewdrops fall,

All: So I know not who came knocking,
At all, at all, at all.

— Walter de la Mare

▶ Read this poem to yourself.

Group 1: Crick! Crack!
Wind at my back.

Group 2: Snit! Snat!
Snatched off my hat.

Group 3: Whew! Whew!
It blew and it blew.

All: Snapped at my ears,
Flapped at my shoes,

And now I've got only
one mitten to lose.

— Eve Merriam

▶ Now read the poem with three different groups. Decide with your group how to say your lines. Talk about the sounds that the words make. Try to make those sounds. Discuss with the class how to read the last four lines.

▶ Draw a picture. Show what you think happened to the other mitten.

▶ **Apply** Choose a poem in this book to read with other classmates. Decide who will read first. Who will read next? Read the poem aloud.

10 Writing a Poem

You have been reading poetry. The poets wrote about things they like to imagine. Now you will be a poet. You will write a poem to share with the class.

1. Prewriting

Writing Project

▶ Your poem will be about you. Imagine that you can be anything you choose. Would you like to be an animal or a mountain? Discuss ideas with a partner.

▶ What will you be in your poem? List words. Tell what you are like. Tell what you can do.

I am an owl.

spooky	shy	hoot
white	howl	glide
wise	wink	peek

2. Writing

▶ Start writing about your topic. Look at your lists. Write down as many ideas as you can. Do not worry if your writing does not look like a poem.

▶ There are many patterns you can use in your poem. Look at these patterns.

You can repeat the same words.

> Night is flying time.
> Night is hunting time.
> Night is my time.
> I am the old barn owl.

You can use words that make special sounds.

> Whoo, whoo, who are you?
> Caw, caw, a friendly crow.
> Bzzz, bzzz, a happy bee.
> Baaa, baaa, a little lamb.

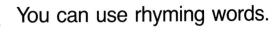

You can use rhyming words.

> I am a nighttime owl.
> I like to hoot and howl.

▶ Now write your poem. Use any pattern you wish. After you write a few lines, stop. Read the lines aloud. Can you hear your pattern?

3. Revising

▶ Read your poem to a classmate. Do you like the way it sounds? Discuss your poem with your classmate. You can ask these questions.

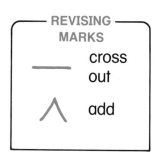

REVISING MARKS

—— cross out

∧ add

- Do I hear a pattern in my poem?

- Did I use adjectives to make my poem interesting?

Look at how Tanya revised her poem.

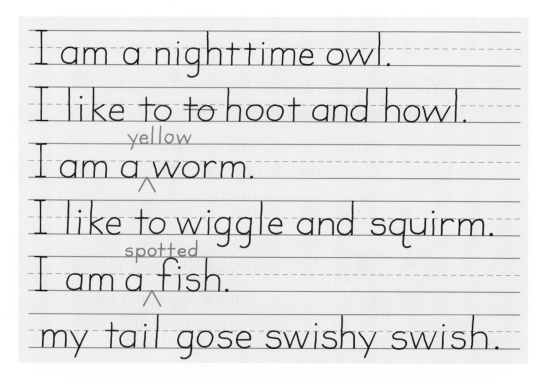

I am a nighttime owl.

I like to ~~to~~ hoot and howl.

I am a ∧yellow worm.

I like to wiggle and squirm.

I am a ∧spotted fish.

my tail gose swishy swish.

▶ Now revise your poem. Use the revising marks to make changes. Try to use adjectives.

4. Publishing

▶ Proofread your poem. Use the proofreading marks to make corrections. These questions will help you proofread.

• Did I spell each word correctly?

• Did I begin each sentence with a capital letter?

• Did I use the correct mark at the end of each sentence?

I am a ^spotted fish.

≡my tail (gose) goes swishy swish.

▶ Practice reading your poem. Try reading with different expressions. Then read your poem into a tape recorder. Enjoy listening to the poems your classmates wrote.

A Poem Mobile

Make a poem mobile.

1. Find a poem you like. It can be one you wrote.
2. Write each line on a piece of heavy paper.
3. Cut the paper into a shape that goes with
   the poem or the line.
4. Hang the lines from a hanger.

Here is what Ann did with a poem she wrote.

> One scarf,
> One hat
> Usually will do.
>
> But for
> mittens and boots,
> You're warmer with two!
>
> —Ann Poole

Science

Writing Poems About the Seasons

Think about summer, fall, winter, and spring.
What does each one look like?
What does each one feel like?
What special things happen in each season?

Choose your favorite season.
Write a poem about it.
This one may give you some ideas.

You know it is the season spring
When baby birds begin to sing.
Your kite flies high,
    like a stretched-out wing.
You hope the wind
    won't break your string.

Adjectives

A. Copy the sentences below. Put a line under the nouns. Circle the adjectives that tell about the nouns.

1. I like sweet apples.
2. She has new skates.
3. They are big birds.
4. We know four songs.
5. He wears brown shoes.
6. I like long sleds.

B. Write the word from each sentence that tells how many.

7. Kurt has two keys.
8. Al reads many books.
9. I see some bluejays.
10. Sara makes one wish.

C. Write the word from each sentence that tells what kind.

11. Carol has straight hair.
12. This plant has tiny flowers.
13. Lee holds an orange balloon.
14. Ted made a round card.

D. Add **-er** or **-est** to the words in ( ).
Then write them for the sentences.

15. Fall is (cold) ___ than spring.
16. Winter is the (cold) ___ season of all.
17. A bear is (tall) ___ than a tiger.
18. A giraffe is the (tall) ___ of all.

Poems

E. Write a word in ( ) to finish each rhyme.

19. It's cool
To jump in a ___. (pool, lake)

20. How neat
To wipe your ___. (hands, feet)

F. Write your own words to finish the poem
below. Use a rhyming word at the end.

Listen to the cool wind blow.
See the little flakes of snow.
Wear your hat and coat today.

_____.

Sentences

A. Write each statement or question correctly.

1. bees make honey
2. did you swim
3. clouds are white
4. how old are you
5. is Rosa home
6. puzzles are fun
7. we saw a fish
8. are you coming

B. Copy the sentences. Circle the naming part. Put a line under the telling part.

9. Jane has dark hair.
10. That chair is old.
11. We walked home.
12. A bus stops here.

Nouns

C. Write the noun in each sentence.

13. The road is bumpy.
14. I live on a farm.
15. The birds flew away.
16. We washed the car.

D. Write the nouns that mean more than one.

17. car	cars	20. tooth	teeth
18. children	child	21. lakes	lake
19. books	book	22. mice	mouse

Verbs

E. Write the correct verb in ( ).

23. Hal (like, likes) art class.
24. Deb (pour, pours) the milk.
25. The boys (need, needs) a ride.
26. The cows (eat, eats) the hay.

F. Add **-ed** to the words in ( ).
Write the new words.

27. The players (kick) the ball.
28. Lisa and Ann (work) hard.
29. I (fix) the old radio.
30. We (sail) on the lake.

Adjectives

G. Write the words that tell
how many or what kind.

31. Beth wears a blue sweater.
32. Richard has three nickels.
33. I see many stars.
34. The pencil has a pointed tip.

A Special Invitation to Books

Little Bear's Friend

by Else Holmelund Minarik

Little Bear and Emily play together all summer. When school starts, Emily has to leave. Little Bear misses her a lot. What can he do?

A Letter to Amy

by Ezra Jack Keats

Peter is having a birthday party. He wants to invite Amy. He writes her a special letter. Something happens on the way to the mailbox.

 ## Dear Garbage Man

by Gene Zion

Sam is a garbage man. He is supposed to throw things away. Sam has a problem. He would rather save things. What can Sam do?

 ## Frog and Toad Are Friends

by Arnold Lobel

In this book you will meet Frog and Toad. You will also learn a lot about best friends. How are you and your friend like Frog and Toad?

 ## How to Find a GOOD Book

What is your favorite holiday? Ask for a book that will tell you more about it.

Thoughts in Bed

Through animal paths in Africa
   The elephant walks alone.
The parrots call in the forest wall
   Of a world that is all their own.

Far above his leafy roof
   A pink flamingo flies.
Great lizards cool their tails in the pool,
   Too lazy to open their eyes.

And when I lie in bed and hear
   The winter winds that come,
When the winter rain on the windowpane
   Is rolling like a drum,

I think of wildest Africa,
   Of jungles yet unknown,
Where the parrots squawk in parrot talk
   And the elephant walks alone.

—Marion Edey

1 Names and Titles for People

- The names of people, pets, and places begin with capital letters.

Program

Boy - tom santos
Girl - judy austin
Dog - spunky
This play takes
place in virginia.

▶ The names in the program should begin with capital letters.
Write the names correctly in the sentences.

1. The dog is played by ___.

2. ___ plays the girl.

3. The boy is played by ___.

4. It takes place in ___.

> Titles for people begin with capital letters. Most titles end with a period.

Mr. Mrs. Ms. Dr. Miss

▶ Look at the titles.
Then write the sentences correctly.

   5. My dentist is dr Roger Turner.

   6. He will visit miss Kane and her class.

   7. Our music teacher is mrs Alice Gray.

   8. Last year ms Edith Matthews taught music.

   9. Did mr Ryan sing a song?

▶ Write the story correctly.

   Visitors came to tell us about their jobs.

dr Sara Chen and ms Linda Rose spoke about

computers. miss Carla Day, mr Jon Allen,

and mrs Fay Silver talked about banking.

2 Titles of Books

> • Begin the first, the last, and all important words in a book title with capital letters.

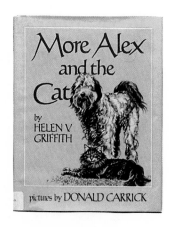

▶ Write the titles correctly.

1. crow boy

2. jack and the beanstalk

3. harry the dirty dog

4. a rainbow of my own

5. katy and the big snow

6. a new day

7. milton the early riser

8. dragon stew

3 Days of the Week

● The names of days of the week begin with capital letters.

On Sunday I skate,
Monday I ride.
On Tuesday I paint,
Wednesday I slide.

On Thursday I jump,
Friday I run.
When Saturday comes,
I have more fun.

There are seven days in a week.
We go to school on five weekdays.

▶ Write answers for the following.

1–2. Which two days are on the weekend?

3–7. Which five days are weekdays?

▶ **Apply** Write about your favorite day of the week. Use the name of the day in your sentence.

4 Months, Holidays, and Special Days

- The names of months, holidays, and special days begin with capital letters.

January	April	July	October
February	May	August	November
March	June	September	December

► Write the month in each pair of sentences correctly.

1. In april, Denver can have snow.
   Phoenix can be hot and sunny.

2. Atlanta has rain in july.
   Los Angeles usually does not.

3. It can be 100°F in Norfolk in september.
   Fairbanks can be 44°F then.

4. Kansas City can be 4°F in january.
   Miami usually is 70°F in that month.

5. In october, Chicago has some rainy days.
   New York City does, too.

These holidays and special days need capital letters.

February

valentine's day
groundhog day

June

father's day
flag day

May

mother's day
memorial day

October

columbus day
halloween

▶ Write the days correctly in the sentences.

People watch for an animal's shadow on __a__. __b__ is in February, too. Mother's Day and __c__ come in May. __d__ and __e__ are in June. Many people make costumes for __f__ but not for __g__.

5 What Is a Pronoun?

> ● A **pronoun** takes the place of a noun.

Lisa and Mike **will plan the party.**
They **will plan the party.**

The word **they** is a pronoun.
It takes the place of the words **Lisa** and **Mike**.

▶ The words **he**, **she**, **it**, **we**, **you**, and **they** are pronouns.
Find the pronouns in the sentences.
Then write them.

1. Last Halloween we had a party.
2. It was a lot of fun.
3. Joan said she remembers the costumes.
4. Do you remember the games?
5. They won the treasure hunt.
6. He got wet bobbing for apples.
7. Did they grow pumpkins?
8. Next year he will be a clown.
9. She will be a lion.
10. Then we will have another party.

▶ Write pronouns for the words in ( ).
Use **He, She, It, They,** or **We.**

11. (The party) ___ is for Valentine's Day.

12. (Pam and Jim) ___ will send invitations.

13. (Tom) ___ will bring food.

14. (Sara) ___ will get balloons.

15. (Mandy and I) ___ are planning games.

16. (John) ___ found a large box.

17. (John and Mike) ___ made a mailbox.

18. (The mailbox) ___ is for Valentine's Day.

19. (Bill and Linda) ___ will deliver the cards.

20. (Our room) ___ is a busy place.

▶ **Apply**   Write two sentences about a party. Use a pronoun in each sentence. Circle the pronouns you use.

6 Using *I* and *me*

- Always write **I** with a capital letter.
- Always name yourself last.

I is used in the naming part of a sentence. The pronoun **me** is used in the telling part.

Bob, Joan, and I like snow.
Kim had a surprise for me.

▶ Write **I** or **me** for each sentence.

1. Kim had a new hat for ___.

2. Sue and ___ made a snowman.

3. Joan helped Bob and ___.

4. My friends and ___ like to skate.

5. Joan and ___ had a race.

6. Bob made hot cocoa for Joan and ___.

7. Then Joan and ___ went home.

7 Using *a* and *an*

- Use **a** if a word begins with a consonant sound.
- Use **an** if a word begins with a vowel sound.

an **inch**

a **foot**

▶ Write **a** or **an** for each sentence.

1. We have ___ math book.

2. This is ___ easy page.

3. Five is ___ odd number.

4. I found ___ good puzzle.

5. It was ___ interesting one.

6. We each made ___ book.

7. Mine had ___ orange cover.

8. Can you add ___ nickel and four dimes?

9. How long is ___ inchworm?

10. Use ___ ruler to find out.

Writing with Pronouns

Grammar and Writing Workshop

• Use pronouns instead of repeating nouns.

A. Joan got the ball and threw the ball.
B. Joan got the ball and threw it.

Both sentences tell the same thing about Joan. Sentence A sounds funny, because the words **the ball** are repeated. Sentence B uses the pronoun **it** instead of **the ball.** When you write, use pronouns instead of repeating nouns.

The Pronoun Game Write each noun. Next to each noun, write the pronoun that can replace it.

1. Mrs. Turner	**a.** they	**5.** Mr. Turner
2. table	**b.** he	**6.** cats and dogs
3. Joe	**c.** it	**7.** Linda
4. Kathy and Jan	**d.** she	**8.** coat

The Pronoun Switch Write a pronoun for the words in ( ). Use words in the Pronoun Bank.

> **Pronoun Bank**
> it we he she they

9. Dee and John hope (Dee and John) ___ can go to the park.
10. Mr. Smith said (Mr. Smith) ___ will coach our team.
11. Linda thinks (Linda) ___ will get a letter.
12. The shoe is so tight that (the shoe) ___ hurts.
13. Bill and I are glad (Bill and I) ___ went on a picnic.

Using the Word Finder Read the paragraph. Then look up **animal** in the Word Finder. Write the names of some animals instead of the word **They**.

When we visited the zoo, all the animals were eating. (They) ___ were eating leaves from tall trees. (They) ___ were roaring and eating meat. (They) ___ were picking up straw with their trunks.

8 Writing an Invitation

▶ Have you ever received an invitation?
Read this invitation.

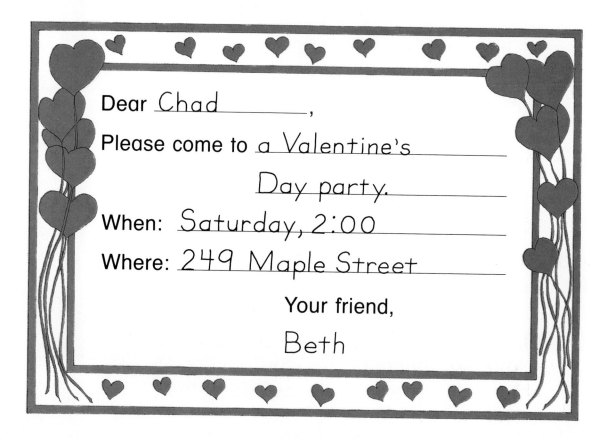

Dear Chad _____ ,

Please come to a Valentine's
            Day party.

When: Saturday, 2:00

Where: 249 Maple Street

                    Your friend,

                    Beth

▶ Write answers for the following questions.

1. Who will receive this invitation?
2. What kind of party will Beth have?
3. When is the party?
4. Where is the party?
5. Who is sending this invitation?

► Copy the invitation below. Fill in the missing parts. Sign your name.

Jessica   a magic show

317 Valley Road   Sunday, 1:30

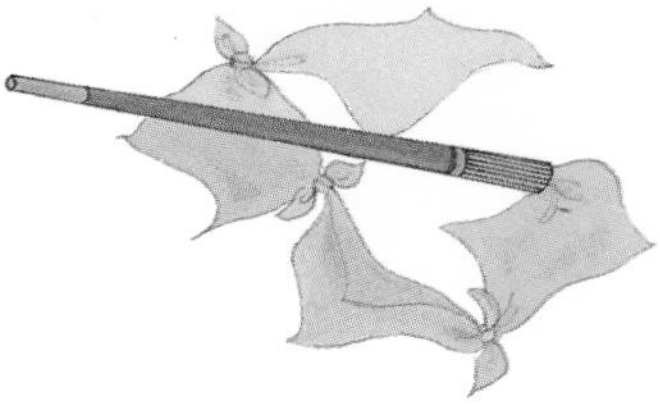

Dear ___ ,

Please come to ___

When: ___

Where: ___

Your friend,

___

9 Parts of a Friendly Letter

▶ A friendly letter has five parts: the **date, greeting, body, closing,** and **signature.**
Read the letter.

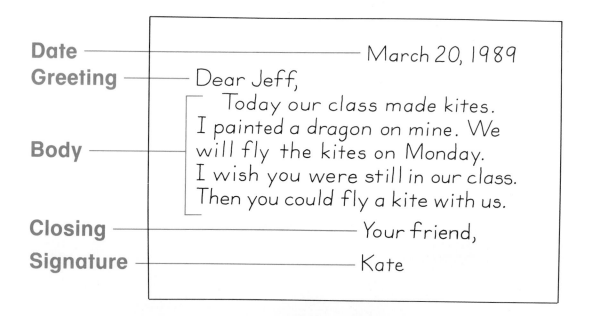

Date ——————————— March 20, 1989
Greeting ——————— Dear Jeff,
Today our class made kites.
Body I painted a dragon on mine. We
will fly the kites on Monday.
I wish you were still in our class.
Then you could fly a kite with us.
Closing ——————— Your friend,
Signature —————— Kate

▶ Write answers for these questions.

1. What is the date?
2. What is the greeting?
3. What is the closing?
4. Who wrote the letter?

Use a **comma** $\boxed{,}$ between the day and the year in the date of a letter. Use a comma after the greeting and the closing. The first words of the greeting and the closing begin with capital letters.

▶ Copy this letter. Write the missing parts. Write today's date. Write a greeting and a closing. Write your own signature. Use commas and capital letters where they belong.

Princess had three puppies yesterday. They are so tiny. The puppies sleep all the time.

▶ **Apply** Write a short letter. Leave out one of the five parts of a friendly letter. Ask a partner to name the part that is missing.

10 Writing a Thank-You Letter

▶ Mrs. Mesa's class went to see the first grade play. The class wrote a thank-you letter. Read their letter.

March 29, 1989

Dear Mr. Bailey's class,
    Thank you for inviting us to your play. You were great actors. We really liked the part when the monkeys took all of the caps.

Your friends,

Mrs. Mesa's class

▶ Copy the beginning of the thank-you letter below. Then finish the letter by writing a few sentences. Thank a friend for doing something for you. Tell why you liked what the person did. Write a closing and sign your name at the end.

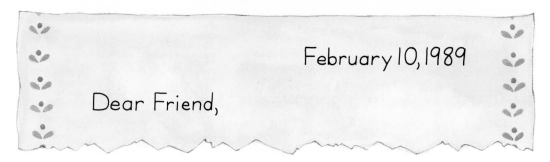

February 10, 1989

Dear Friend,

11 Addressing an Envelope

▶ Look at the envelope. Find the address. It tells who will receive the letter. Find the return address. It tells who is sending the letter.

Return address

Mr. Scott Barnes
201 Apple Street
Atlanta, Georgia 30305

Address

Jan Bolla
2016 Daisy Road
Chicago, Illinois 60614

▶ Tell who will receive the letter. Tell who is sending the letter.

▶ **Apply** Get an envelope or draw one on a sheet of paper. Then address the envelope to a friend. You may make up your friend's address. Use your own return address.

12 Writing a Friendly Letter

Writing Project

Everyone likes to receive letters. Who would enjoy hearing from you? You will write a letter to send to that person.

1. Prewriting

▶ Think of all the people to whom you could write. It may be a friend. It may be someone in your family. You can write a letter to anyone you choose. Finish this sentence.

I will write a letter to _____.

▶ What will you write about in your letter? Discuss ideas with your classmates. Your teacher will make a list of your ideas.

my pet
a family trip
a special event
a new game
a favorite book

▶ Think about each idea on the list. Which one interests you? Choose your favorite idea. This is your topic. Write a sentence that tells what you will write about.

Paul made this question chart. It helped him think about what to say in his letter. He answered questions about his topic.

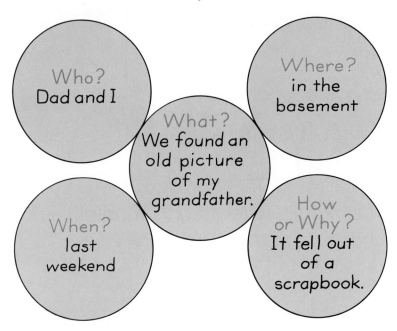

Who?
Dad and I

Where?
in the
basement

What?
We found an
old picture
of my
grandfather.

When?
last
weekend

How
or Why?
It fell out
of a
scrapbook.

▶ Make a question chart before you write your letter. Write **What?** in the middle circle. Answer the question. This is your topic. Write other question words. Put one in each circle. Then answer the questions. They will help you think about your topic.

2. Writing

▶ Writing a letter is like talking to a person. Write a letter to the person you chose. Use your question chart to help you.

3. Revising

▶ Read your letter to a classmate. Does your classmate understand what you wrote? Ask yourself these questions.

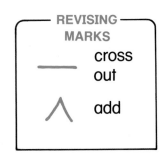

REVISING MARKS

— cross out

∧ add

- Does my letter say what I mean?

- Did I tell enough about my topic?

- Will my reader enjoy this letter?

Here is a part of Paul's letter to his grandfather. Look at the changes he made when he revised.

Dad and I were cleaning.

We found an old scrappbook.

A picture fell out.
It was you when you were a

little boy. you looked like me!

your   in the picture
Was that Grandpa's pony?

▶ Now revise your letter. Use the revising marks.

4. Publishing

▶ Proofread your letter. Use the proofreading marks to make corrections. These questions will help you proofread.

PROOFREADING MARKS

⬭ check spelling

≡ capital letter

- Did I spell each word correctly?

- Did I begin each sentence with a capital letter?

- Did I use the correct mark at the end of each sentence?

> scrapbook
>
> We found an old scrappbook.
> A picture fell out.
> It was you when you were a
> little boy. you looked like me!

▶ Make a neat copy of your letter. Address an envelope and put your letter inside. Mail your letter or deliver it in person. Someone will enjoy hearing from you.

My Own Stationery

There are many different ways to make your own stationery. Here is one way.

1. Get paper, an empty spool of thread, and some paint.
2. Dip one end of the spool into one color of paint. Dip the other end into another color.
3. Start at a corner of the paper. Put the spool down on the paper. Hold the middle of the spool, where there isn't any paint. Roll it along the edge of the paper.
4. You can make straight lines. You can make wavy lines. You can roll it along, then stop for a while.

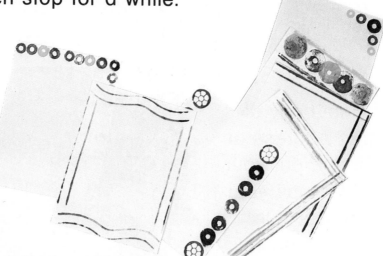

Science

Clean air, water, and land are important for living things. Many people work hard to keep your town clean. Do you know anyone who has helped your town? Did anyone clean up a stream or a park? Did a neighborhood group do something special? Try to find out. Then give that person or group a big "thank-you."

Apply   Write a thank-you letter to a person or group who has done something special.

- Use the stationery you made yourself.
- Remember to use the five parts of a letter.
- Write the address and return address on an envelope.
- After you proofread your work, mail the letter.

Building Bridges

Nouns

A. Write each name or title correctly.

1. mr joe mills   **3.** december

2. stone soup   **4.** georgia

Pronouns

B. Write **He, She, It,** or **We** for the words in (   ).

5. (Rick) is late.   **7.** (Sue and I) run.
6. (The airplane) flies.   **8.** (Mary) makes toys.

C. Write **I** or **me** for each sentence.

9. Dan and (I, me) play catch.
10. Len drew a picture of (I, me).
11. Amy helped Pat and (I, me).
12. Tom and (I, me) saw an owl.

A and *An*

D. Write **a** or **an** for each sentence.

13. Peg told us ___ funny story.
14. Ramon needs ___ alarm clock.
15. Ms. Wong planted ___ oak tree.

Letters

E. Read the invitation. Write the answer to each question.

Dear Tammy_____,
Please come to _a picnic._
When: _April 9, 3:00_
Where: _Sheldon Park_

Your friend,
David

16. Who is invited?
17. What is she invited to?
18. When is it?
19. Where is it?
20. Who sent the invitation?

F. Match the parts of the letter to their names.

21. March 1, 1989   **a.** greeting
22. Dear Jack,   **b.** signature
23. Your friend,   **c.** date
24. Benjamin   **d.** closing

A Special Invitation to Books

Emma

by Wendy Kesselman

Emma gets a painting for her birthday. It shows the village where she grew up. Emma remembers her village differently, so she buys her own paints and becomes an artist.

Look Again

by Tana Hoban

You will want to look closely at the photographs in this book. You see only a part of a picture on each page. You guess what the picture is. Then you can lift the page to see if you are right.

Guess What

by Beau Gardner

This book plays a guessing game with you. First you see part of an animal. You guess what the animal is. Then you turn the page for the answer.

Use Your Head, Dear

by Aliki

Charles is an alligator who cannot remember anything. He gets things mixed up. He forgets what he is doing. Then his father gives him a perfect present.

How to Find a GOOD Book

Read the book jacket before you choose a book. The jacket cover will tell you what the book is about.

Tails

A dog's tail
     is short
And a cat's tail
     is long,
And a horse has a tail
     that he
     swishes along,
And a fish has a tail
     that can
     help him
     to swim,
And a pig has a tail
     that looks
     curly on him.
All monkeys have tails
And the elephants too.

There are
hundreds of
tails
if
  you
    look
      in
        the
         zoo!

—*Myra Cohn Livingston*

1 Using *is* and *are*

Now	One	is
	More than one	are

Our teacher is kind.   **It is a game.**
Jo and I are friends.   **We are happy.**

▶ Read the sentences above.
Then write **is** or **are** for each sentence below.

1. The Science Fair ___ today.

2. This chart ___ mine.

3. They ___ footprints.

4. These magnets ___ strong.

5. The cork ___ light.

6. We ___ very busy at the fair.

7. Many things ___ on display.

8. My friend ___ good at science.

9. Science ___ my favorite subject.

10. The fair ___ very exciting.

2 Using *was* and *were*

In the Past	One	was
	More than one	were

The dinosaur was big.   **It was long ago.**
The boys were on time.   **They were here.**

▶ Read the sentences above.
Then write **was** or **were** for each sentence below.

1. The Science Fair ___ last week.

2. Two reporters ___ there.

3. Our pictures ___ in the paper.

4. My chart ___ in one picture.

5. We ___ very excited.

6. It ___ lots of fun.

7. We ___ surprised!

8. Our teacher ___ surprised, too.

9. I ___ glad my family came.

10. They ___ glad, too.

3 Using *has* and *have*

Now	One	has
	More than one	have

Roberto has fun.   **She has a cat.**
Mary and Ted have books.   **We have brothers.**

▶ Read the sentences above.
Then write **has** or **have** for each sentence below.

1. We ___ a special park in town.

2. It ___ lots of rides.

3. Tim and I ___ tickets.

4. Molly ___ her sister with her.

5. They ___ a magician this year.

6. The magician ___ a rabbit in a hat.

7. One booth ___ rings to toss.

8. Another one ___ balloons.

9. We ___ a roller coaster there, too.

10. All of us ___ fun at the park.

4 Using *come* and *run*

Now	come, comes	run, runs
In the Past	came	ran

Today we come to school. **Now Alice runs fast.**
Yesterday Larry came, too. **Last week she ran a race.**

▶ Read the sentences above.
Then write the correct word from each ( ) below.

1. Last year Jenny (runs, ran) in the race.

2. She ran and (comes, came) in first.

3. We (come, came) to see her often now.

4. Now many people (run, ran) in races.

5. My brother (comes, came) now, too.

6. He warms up and (runs, ran).

7. My dog (comes, came) and watches.

8. Last week I (run, ran) a mile.

5 Using *give* and *take*

Now	give, gives	take, takes
In the Past	gave	took

Today we give a party.   **Joe takes piano lessons.**
Last week Sara gave a gift.   **Yesterday they took a walk.**

▶ Read the sentences above.
Then write the correct word from each ( ) below.

1. Last week David (gives, gave) me a birdhouse.

2. Now I (give, gave) seeds to the birds.

3. One bird comes and (takes, took) the most.

4. Yesterday it (takes, took) bread crumbs.

5. Now it comes and (gives, gave) some to its babies.

6. Today squirrels come and (take, took) seeds.

6 Using *do* and *go*

Now	do, does	go, goes
In the Past	did	went

Today I do the dishes.   **She goes with me now.**
Yesterday Ed did the puzzle.   **Last week they went away.**

▶ Read the sentences above.
Then write the correct word from each ( ) below.

1. Years ago some people (do, did) a brave thing.

2. Long ago they (go, went) to the North Pole.

3. People still (go, went) and visit there.

4. A person walks or (goes, went) by dogsled.

5. Who (does, did) things like that now?

6. People travel and (do, did) exciting things.

7 Contractions

- A **contraction** is a short way to put words together.
- An **apostrophe** ['] takes the place of one or more letters.

The tulips are not **open yet.**
The tulips aren't **open yet.**

The word **aren't** is a contraction.
It is a short way of putting **are** and **not** together.
An apostrophe takes the place of **o** in **not**.

▶ Match the words with their contractions.

1. is not	**a.** aren't	**6.** has not	**f.** couldn't
2. are not	**b.** doesn't	**7.** have not	**g.** wouldn't
3. do not	**c.** isn't	**8.** could not	**h.** hasn't
4. does not	**d.** didn't	**9.** would not	**i.** shouldn't
5. did not	**e.** don't	**10.** should not	**j.** haven't

▶ **Apply** Write contractions for the words in ( ).

11. I (did not) ___ see the rainbow.
12. I just (could not) ___ find it.
13. I (have not) ___ ever seen one.

8 Contractions

We will use a computer today.
We'll use a computer today.

The word **we'll** is a contraction for **we will**.
An apostrophe takes the place of **wi** in **will**.

▶ Match the words with their contractions.

1. I will	**a.** she'll	**6.** I am	**f.** we're
2. he will	**b.** they'll	**7.** he is	**g.** I'm
3. she will	**c.** I'll	**8.** she is	**h.** she's
4. we will	**d.** he'll	**9.** we are	**i.** they're
5. they will	**e.** we'll	**10.** they are	**j.** he's

▶ **Apply**   Write contractions for the words in ( ).

11. (I am) ___ excited about computers.
12. (We are) ___ using one for English.
13. Tomorrow (you are) ___ going to try it.
14. I think (it is) ___ fun to use.

Writing with Verbs

• Stay in the same time when you write.

A. Carla **came** to visit.
She **gave** me a kite.

B. I **came** home.
Then I **go** out to play.

Which pair of sentences sounds better? Pair A does, because the verbs **came** and **gave** tell about the same time. They both tell about the past.

The verbs in pair B tell about now and the past. They are in different times. When you write, keep your verbs in the same time.

The Verb Game 1–14. The words in the Verb Bank tell about now and the past. Write the word **Now** on your paper. Write all the verbs that tell about now under it. Then write **In the Past** on your paper. Write all the verbs that tell about the past under it.

Verb Bank						
is	ran	do	went	come	was	did
go	were	are	came	give	run	gave

The Verb Switch   Write the story below.
Make all the verbs tell about the past.

Josie had a special day. She goes to
the station. Her uncle is on the train.
When he came out, Josie runs to him.
She gives him a hug.

Using the Word Finder   Look up **go** in the
Word Finder. Read each sentence below.
If you find a better word than **go,** write it.
If you do not find one that is better, write **go.**

15. We go on our bikes.
16. They go in the relay race.
17. Did you go in the plane?
18. I can go over the log.
19. A green light tells us to go.

9 Remembering

Thinking Skills

You have already learned many things. You can remember many important facts. Sometimes remembering is easy. Sometimes it is difficult.

▶ Write answers to these questions.
What answers can you remember easily?

1. What is the name of one fruit?
2. What are the names of two wild animals?
3. What are the names of three famous people?

▶ Does everyone remember the same things? Find out. Follow these steps.

Step 1: Look at the picture on the next page.

Step 2: Close your book. Try to remember the picture. Then make a list of all the things in the picture.

Step 3: Tell a partner what things you remembered. Is your partner's list the same as yours? Look at the picture again. Circle the things you both forgot to list.

▶ **Close your book and try again.** See if you can remember more about the picture. Add new things to your list.

You as a Thinker

- How do you remember? Tell about how you remembered the picture in this lesson.

- When do you need to remember? Tell about one time when looking again can help you.

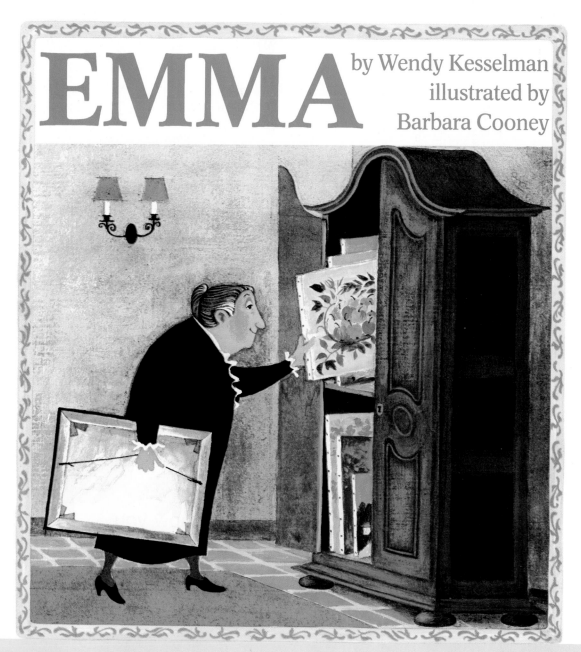

EMMA

by Wendy Kesselman
illustrated by
Barbara Cooney

It was Emma's birthday.
She was seventy-two years old.

Emma had four children,
seven grandchildren,
and fourteen great grandchildren.

Emma was happy when her family came to visit.
She baked noodle puddings and chocolate cream pies.
She put flowers everywhere.

Her family brought her lots of presents,
but they never stayed very long.

So most of the time Emma was all alone.
And sometimes she was very lonely.

The only company she had was her orange cat,
Pumpkinseed.
They sat together outside
and curled their toes in the sun.
They listened to the woodpecker
tapping at the old apple tree.

Sometimes Pumpkinseed got stuck at the top of the tree,
and Emma had to climb up and rescue him.
But Emma didn't mind.
She loved climbing trees.

She loved all kinds of simple things.

She loved to see the snow
come right up to her doorstep.

She loved to sit and dream about the little village
across the mountains where she grew up.

But when she told her family about the things
she loved, they laughed and said to each other,
"Poor Emma. She must be getting old."

For her seventy-second birthday the family gave Emma
a painting of her little village across the mountains.

Emma hung the painting on the wall.
"It's beautiful," she said to them.
But to herself she thought,
"That's not how I remember my village at all."

Every day Emma looked at the painting and frowned.
And every day her frown grew a little deeper.

One day she made up her mind.

She went to the store and bought paints and
brushes and an easel.

Then Emma sat by the window and painted her village
just the way she remembered it.

When it was finished she took the other painting
off the wall and hung hers up instead.

And every day Emma looked at her painting and smiled.

When her family came to visit,
Emma put the other painting back again.
And as soon as they left she switched it for her own.

But one day Emma forgot.

When the family was in the middle of dinner,
one of Emma's grandchildren pointed to the wall.
"Where did that painting come from?
It's not the one we gave you!"

Emma looked up. Emma looked down.
But everyone kept right on looking at the painting,
and they all kept asking,
"Yes, where did it come from?"

Finally Emma said, "Me," very softly. "*I* did it."

"*You!*" they all cried out together.

Emma hurried to hide the painting in the closet.

"Stop!" cried her family. "Don't hide it away!"
"It's beautiful! Why don't you paint another one?"

"I have," said Emma.
And she brought twenty more paintings
out of the closet.

From that day Emma kept painting
and she never stopped.
She painted the snow coming right up to her doorstep.

She painted the old apple tree in blossom
with the woodpecker tapping at its branches.

She painted Pumpkinseed curling his toes in the sun.

And she painted her village across the mountains
over and over and over again.

Soon people began coming from everywhere
to look at Emma's paintings.
When they left she was all alone.

But now Emma had something else.
She sat by the window every day and painted
from morning till night.
She painted hundreds of paintings.

Her paintings covered the walls.
They filled the closets.
They hung in the kitchen cupboards.

Emma was surrounded by the friends and places
she loved. And she was never lonely again.

Talking About the Story

What do you remember about Emma? Draw Emma. Write sentences about Emma on your picture.

You as a Reader

1. Emma loved her village. Draw a picture. Show a place you love.

2. Why did Emma hide her paintings?

3. Emma painted her village over and over again. Tell what you like to do over and over again.

You as a Writer

What do you remember about a special place? What would you write about it?

11 Finding the Main Idea

The sentences below are all about one idea. That idea is called the **main idea.** The main idea is <u>Emma painted hundreds of paintings.</u>

Emma painted hundreds of paintings. Her paintings covered the walls. They filled the closets. They hung in the kitchen cupboards.

▶ Read the sentences below.
Write the sentence that tells the main idea.

1. Grandma Moses was an important painter. She started painting when she was 76 years old. Her colorful pictures show farms and small towns. Many people enjoy her work.

- Many people enjoy her work.
- Grandma Moses was an important painter.
- She started painting when she was 76 years old.

▶ Read each group of sentences below.
Write the main idea.

2.   My grandmother is a busy person. She writes stories for the newspaper. Every Monday she goes to meetings. At home she grows vegetables in her garden.

3.   My grandmother is like Emma. She likes to bake for us. She loves our visits. My grandmother even has a cat.

4.   We are having a birthday party for my grandmother. It will be a surprise. Everyone in the family will be there. There will be lots of food to eat. Uncle Vic is going to take pictures.

▶ **Apply**   Turn back to the story. Read page 178.
Tell the main idea in your own words.

12 Finding Details

A **detail** gives information. A detail tells more about the main idea. There may be more than one detail in a group of sentences.

▶ Read the group of sentences below. The main idea is <u>Emma had a cat</u>. The other sentences are details. They tell about Emma's cat.

> Emma had a cat. His name was Pumpkinseed. Emma's cat was orange. He kept Emma company.

▶ **1–2.** Read this group of sentences about Emma. The main idea is <u>Emma was happy when her family came to visit</u>. Write the details that tell about the main idea.

> Emma was happy when her family came to visit. She baked noodle puddings and chocolate cream pies. She put flowers everywhere.

▶ **3.** Read this group of sentences from <u>Emma</u>. Write the main idea.

> She loved all kinds of simple things. She loved to see the snow come right up to her doorstep. She loved to sit and dream about the little village across the mountains where she grew up.

▶ **4–5.** Write details that tell about the main idea. Use your own words.

▶ **Apply** Turn back to the story. It begins on page 174. Find details that show how Emma was a special person. Read the details to your classmates.

13 Writing Main Idea and Details

▶ Read this main idea.

Emma and Pumpkinseed were friends.

▶ Read these details. Some tell more about the main idea. Some do not tell about the main idea.

They liked to sit together outside.

Emma was seventy-two years old.

They listened to the woodpecker tapping in the tree.

Emma dreamed about the village where she grew up.

▶ Find the details that tell about the main idea. Write the main idea. Then write the details.

▶ Read these main idea sentences. Each one tells about the picture. Which main idea do you like best? Write the sentence. Then write details that tell more about the main idea.

The boys like to be together.

The boys are best friends.

The boys have fun together.

▶ Write a main idea. Tell about you and your friend.

▶ Write details. Tell more about your main idea.

14 Writing About Something I Remember

Writing Project

In the story you read, Emma liked to remember her village. What do you like to remember?

You will write a story about something you like to remember. You can share your story with your family and your classmates.

1. Prewriting

▶ Make an idea cluster. Write **I like to remember** in the middle circle. Draw more circles. Write something you like to remember in each circle.

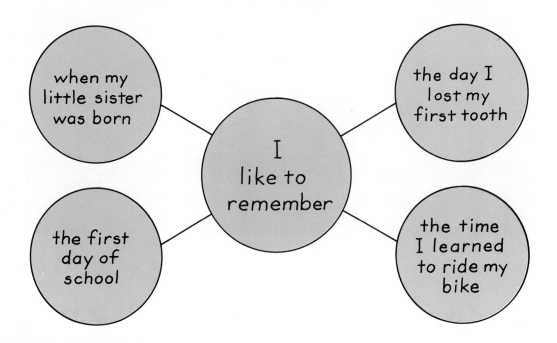

when my little sister was born

the day I lost my first tooth

I like to remember

the first day of school

the time I learned to ride my bike

► Look at your cluster. Think about your ideas.
Choose one idea to write about. This is your topic.

► Tell a classmate about the topic you chose.
Ask your classmate, "What do you want to know
more about?" Together make a question list.

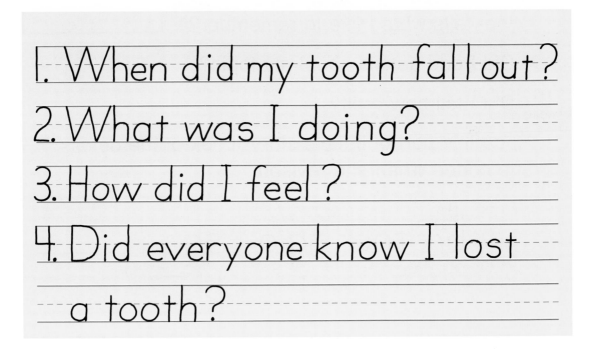

1. When did my tooth fall out?
2. What was I doing?
3. How did I feel?
4. Did everyone know I lost
   a tooth?

2. Writing

► How should you begin your writing? Write
a sentence. Tell what you like to remember.

► Look at your question list. As you write, you
may wish to answer the questions. Your
answers will help you tell more about your topic.

3. Revising

▶ Read your story to a partner.
Does your partner understand your
writing? Answer these questions.

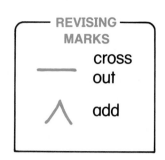

- Did I begin with a sentence
  that tells what I like to remember?

- Did I add details about my topic?

- Did I tell how I felt?

Read this part of Jana's story. Look at the details
she added when she revised.

> my brother said I shud
> eat ~~a~~ an apple I took one ∧huge bite.
> Then my ∧wiggly tooth fell out. I
> felt very grown up and excited
> when I lost my first tooth.

▶ Now revise your writing. Use the revising marks
to make changes.

4. Publishing

▶ Proofread your writing. Use the proofreading marks to make corrections. These questions will help you proofread.

- Did I spell each word correctly?

- Did I begin each sentence with a capital letter?

- Did I use the correct mark at the end of each sentence?

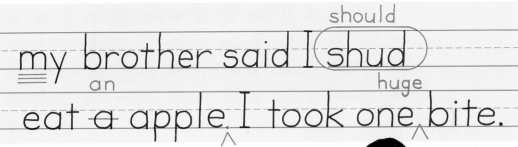

my brother said I shud (should)

eat a apple. I took one bite. (an) (huge)

▶ Make a neat copy of your story. Draw a picture to go with your story. Read your story to your family. Ask them what they remember about the time you wrote about.

A Memory Book

A memory is something that you remember. A memory may be about a person, a place, a thing, or an event. You can make a memory book to remember special things.

1. Get several pieces of heavy paper.
2. Punch three holes in one side of the papers.
3. Tie all the pages together with yarn.
4. Begin collecting things to put in your memory book. You may want to save a ticket from the circus. You may save a card or a photo from your birthday.
5. Cut out or draw pictures for your memory book. You can write in your book, too.

Art

Look at the picture. Can you tell what animal the picture shows? How do you know? How is the picture like the real animal? How is it different?

Pablo Picasso. *Bird on a Tree.* August 1928. Oil on canvas, 13¾" x 9½". **Photo:** Carmelo Guadagno. The Justin K. Thannhauser Collection; Solomon R. Guggenheim Foundation, New York.

Apply Draw a picture of the same animal. How is your drawing the same as the picture on this page? How is your picture different? How is your drawing the same as the real animal? How is it different?

Verbs

A. Write the correct word in ( )
for each sentence.

1. Jill (is, are) my friend.
2. Bears (is, are) big animals.
3. We (was, were) very hungry.
4. Bobby (was, were) asleep.
5. They (has, have) two dogs.
6. Cal (has, have) gray eyes.

B. Write the correct word in ( ).

7. Yesterday Kate (runs, ran) in the race.
8. We (come, came) to every game now.
9. Last week Matt (takes, took) my picture.
10. Pat bakes pies and (gives, gave) them to us.
11. Now the cows (go, went) into the barn.
12. Fred and I (do, did) the puzzle last night.

C. Match the words with their contractions.

13. is not	**a.** don't	**16.** I will	**d.** it's
14. has not	**b.** isn't	**17.** we are	**e.** we're
15. do not	**c.** hasn't	**18.** it is	**f.** I'll

Main Idea and Details

D. Read each group of sentences. Write the sentence that tells the main idea.

19.   I like to play the drums. I have a lesson every Tuesday. Someday I will be in a band.

20.   Al wanted a pet. He read books about pets. He asked his friends about pets.

21.   Tina saw a butterfly. It flew over her head. Then it landed on a flower.

22.   Sports are fun to play. Some people like to play soccer. Other people like softball best.

E. Read the group of sentences below. Follow the directions.

It rained all day. There were big puddles in the street. Everyone carried an umbrella. I wore my yellow boots.

23. Write the sentence that tells the main idea.

24–25. Write two details that tell about the main idea.

A Special Invitation to Books

Hold My Hand
by Charlotte Zolotow

Two little girls are outside. The sky gets dark. The wind sighs. It is cold, cold, cold. Snow falls. Holding hands makes the day seem warmer.

A Day of Summer
by Betty Miles

Summer has its own noises. It has special smells and special colors. It has its own tastes. When you read this book, you will see and feel summer.

Gilberto and the Wind
by Marie Hall Ets

Gilberto describes how he plays with the wind. He feels it blow. He sees it move things. Sometimes soft, sometimes strong, the wind is his friend.

Dawn
by Uri Shulevitz

Have you ever been to the country? Have you ever watched the sun rise? A new day begins. You see and hear the country wake up in this book.

How to Find a GOOD Book
Do you like riddles and jokes? Your library has whole books of them.

My Dog

My dog can walk,
My dog can run.
My dog can bark
Just for fun.

My dog sits up
And begs to play,
He shakes my hand
Then runs away.

—*Lois Lenski*

1 Words That Tell *When* and *Where*

> ● An **adverb** tells more about a verb.

We look up at the red light.
It changes now.

An adverb can tell **when** or **where.**
The word **up** tells **where** we look.
The word **now** tells **when** the light changes.

▶ Copy the sentences below.
Put a line under each verb.
Circle each adverb that tells when or where.

1. We will walk today.
2. I always go with my friends.
3. We wait here.
4. The green light changes soon.
5. We look around.
6. The children walk across.

▶ Write the adverbs.
Write **when** if the adverb tells when.
Write **where** if the adverb tells where.

7. I never forget my homework.
8. I work inside.
9. My friends play here.
10. We always have fun.
11. We sometimes play tag.
12. We run around.
13. We made kites yesterday.
14. Today we fly them.
15. My kite falls there.
16. The other kites stay up.
17. We like to play outdoors.

▶ **Apply** Write two sentences about something you like to do. Use adverbs that tell when and where. Circle the adverbs.

2 Words That Tell *How*

We plant the garden carefully.

The word **carefully** is an adverb.
It tells **how** we plant the garden.

▶ Copy the sentences below.
Circle the adverbs that tell how.

1. We neatly rake the garden.
2. My brother works quickly.
3. He finishes nicely.
4. We firmly cover the seeds.
5. It rains lightly.
6. Our plants grow slowly.
7. We carefully pull out weeds.
8. We look proudly at our garden.

3 The Suffix *-ly*

> • A **suffix** is a letter or letters added to the end of a word.

soft + ly = softly

▶ Add **-ly** to the words in ( ).
Then write them for the sentences.

1. We hide (quiet) ___ .
2. Maria counts (loud) ___ .
3. She looks for us (clever) ___ .
4. We peek (slow) ___ .
5. We run (light) ___ .
6. Then we run (quick) ___ .
7. Did you have a turn (late) ___ ?
8. Some people count (different) ___ .

▶ **Apply**   Add **-ly** to **part** and **night**.
Write a sentence for each new word.

4 The Suffixes *-ful* and *-less*

Suffix	Meaning	Example
-ful -less	full of without	care + ful = careful spot + less = spotless

colorless

colorful

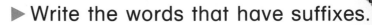
▶ Write the words that have suffixes.

1. Your puppy is playful.
2. It is fearless.
3. We like to be helpful.
4. Ted is breathless.
5. This is a wonderful story.
6. We feel joyful.

▶ Add **-ful** or **-less** to the words in ( ).
Write them for the sentences.

7. It is (thought) ___ to be kind.
8. The lost dog is (home) ___ now.
9. A good sleep is (rest) ___.
10. Be (care) ___ crossing the street.

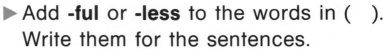

5 Words That Sound Alike

> • Some words sound alike but have different meanings and spellings.

We see **the plane fly over the** sea.

The words **see** and **sea** sound alike.
They have different meanings and spellings.

▶ Write the two words in each sentence that sound alike.

1. We rode our bikes on that road.
2. I won a prize one time.
3. Did you read two books, too?
4. I can hear you from here.
5. We ate all eight apples.
6. Can you write a story right now?

Writing with Adverbs

> ● Use adverbs to make your writing more interesting.

A. Tom ran.

B. Today Tom ran there swiftly.

Both sentences above tell that Tom ran. Sentence B tells more. It tells <u>when</u>, <u>where</u>, and <u>how</u> Tom ran. **Today, there,** and **swiftly** tell more about what Tom did. When you write, use adverbs to make your writing more interesting.

The Adverb Game   Find the adverbs that are hidden in the puzzle. Write one for each verb.

1. whisper ___

2. write ___

3. ride ___

4. end ___

5. play ___

6. come ___

s	q	u	a	s	h	h
o	u	t	s	i	d	e
o	i	n	k	t	o	r
n	e	a	t	l	y	e
a	t	o	d	a	y	a
l	l	n	k	d	o	t
l	y	e	s	d	u	e

Add-an-Adverb Make the sentences below more interesting. Add an adverb from the Adverb Bank to each sentence.

> **Adverb Bank**
> tomorrow   always   down   quickly

7. Tulips grow ___ .
8. Let's go to the library ___ .
9. Please climb ___ .
10. I ___ loved painting.

Using the Word Finder Read the paragraph. Then look up **well** in the Word Finder. If you find a better word for **well**, write it. If you do not find one that is better, write **well**.

Sue swims (**11.** well) ___ . She moves (**12.** well) ___ in the water. She dives (**13.** well) ___ , too. Sue thinks (**14.** well) ___ before she dives. When she won the meet, she swam (**15.** well) ___ .

6 What Is a Paragraph?

A **paragraph** is a group of sentences about one main idea. One sentence tells the main idea. The other sentences add details about it.

The first word in a paragraph is **indented.** That means it is moved in a little to the right. The other sentences are not indented. They do not have to start on a new line.

▶ Read this paragraph.

Neal is interested in fish. He has a fish tank in his room. He watches his fish closely. He is learning to take care of them.

1. Write the sentence that tells the main idea.
2. Write the word that is indented.

▶ Read this paragraph.

Fish have different shapes. Some fish look like bumpy rocks. Others look like wiggly worms. There are even fish as flat as pancakes.

3. Write the sentence that tells the main idea.
4. Write a sentence that gives a detail about the main idea.

Sentences in a paragraph must be written in order. If they are not, the paragraph will not make sense.

▶ Read these sentences.
They are not in paragraph order.

> Then he filled it with water. First he got a large tank. Last he put in some colorful fish. Carlos wanted some pet fish.

5. Write the sentence that should come first in the paragraph.

6. Write the sentence that should come last in the paragraph.

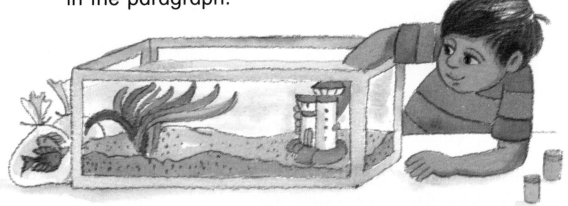

▶ **Apply** Write the sentences below in a paragraph. Put the sentences in the best order.

> Jill has a pet fish.
> Gus is a guppy.
> His name is Gus.
> A guppy is a tropical fish.

7 Keeping to One Topic

The main idea is the topic of a paragraph. Every sentence in a paragraph should keep to the topic.

▶ Read the paragraph. Which sentence does not keep to the topic? Write it.

A baby elephant was born at the zoo. She weighed 210 pounds. The workers at the zoo were excited about the baby elephant. They named her Marigold. The seal's name was Palmer.

▶ Write the paragraph. Leave out the sentence that does not keep to the topic. Remember to indent the paragraph.

Sometimes animals in a zoo get sick. Most zoos have an animal doctor. Children can pet the animals in a petting zoo. The doctor helps the animals get well.

8 Telling Enough

When you write a paragraph, be sure you tell enough. What else would the reader like to know? Try to answer the reader's questions.

▶ Read this paragraph. It does not tell enough. What else do you want to know?

The contest was exciting. Children entered the contest. They had to do something. A second grader won. She won a prize.

▶ Write the paragraph. Use your own words to make the paragraph tell enough. The questions will help you tell more.

The ____What kind?____ contest was exciting.

____How many?____ children entered the contest.

They had to ____What did they do?____. A second grader

won. She won a ____What?____.

9

Writing Descriptive Details

Everyone enjoys the picnic.

▶ The sentence below the picture tells the main idea. Now write other sentences that give details about the picnic. Tell how things look, sound, smell, feel, and taste.

1. Tell how something looks.
2. Tell how something sounds.
3. Tell how something smells.
4. Tell how something feels.
5. Tell how something tastes.

▶ Read this paragraph.

> We kept walking until we came to an old barn. The red paint was chipped. The heavy door creaked. It was empty and quiet inside. The barn smelled like hay.

The first sentence in the paragraph tells what the paragraph is about. It is about a barn. The other sentences describe the barn. They tell what the barn looked like. They tell how the door sounded. They tell how the barn smelled. The sentences give many descriptive details.

▶ **6.** Look at the picture. Write a sentence that tells the main idea.

▶ **7–8.** Write two descriptive details that tell more about the main idea.

10

Writing About My Favorite Place

Writing Project

Look at Todd's tree house. It is his favorite place. He likes to watch the squirrels and listen to a woodpecker knocking.

Everyone has a favorite place. Sarah likes the top of the bunk bed. Juan likes the part of the basement where he builds his models. You can write about your favorite place. You can share your writing with the class.

1. Prewriting

▶ Draw a picture of your favorite place. Show what you like to do there.

▶ Make a list of words that tell about your favorite place. Ask yourself, "What do I see, hear, feel, smell, and taste in my favorite place?"

2. Writing

▶ Think about how you will begin your paragraph. Read these sentence starters. If you wish, choose one for your first sentence.

- My favorite place is ___.
- I like my favorite place because ___.
- When I am in my favorite place ___.

▶ Write a paragraph about your favorite place. Begin with the sentence starter you chose. Use your list of words to help you write descriptive details. Your picture will give you ideas to write about, too.

3. Revising

▶ Read your paragraph aloud. Ask a classmate to listen. Talk about ways you can revise your writing.

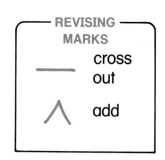

REVISING MARKS

—— cross out

∧ add

- Are all my sentences about my favorite place?

- Did I write descriptive details?

- Does my writing make sense?

Read Todd's paragraph. He crossed out a sentence that did not tell about his favorite place.

My favorite place is my tree
house. i like to ~~see~~ the   watch
squirls chaseing each other.
I see ∧ houses. ~~Peter is my best~~   the tops of
~~friend.~~ Jets fly over my tree ∧.   zoom   house

▶ Now revise your paragraph. Make the changes you and your classmate discussed.

4. Publishing

▶ Proofread your paragraph. Use the proofreading marks to make corrections. These questions will help you proofread.

PROOFREADING MARKS

¶   indent

◯   check spelling

≡   capital letter

- Did I indent the first word?

- Did I spell each word correctly?

- Did I begin each sentence with a capital letter?

- Did I use the correct end marks?

¶ My favorite place is my tree house. i like to ~~see~~ watch the ~~squirls~~ squirrels ~~chaseing~~ chasing each other.

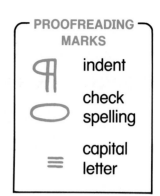

▶ Copy your paragraph. Hang a picture of your favorite place on the bulletin board. Read your paragraph to the class. Have your classmates guess which picture is yours.

A Funny Animal

You can make real or make-believe animal statues.

1. Get some boxes, cardboard tubes, glue, tape, paint, and scissors.
2. Decide what you want to make.
3. Glue and tape your boxes and tubes together.
4. Paint your animal.
5. Write a paragraph that describes what you have made. Do not tell what it is. Write about its size, shape, and color. Write what it can do.
6. Everyone will get someone else's paragraph. All of the animals will be on a table or shelf together.
7. Read the paragraph you are given. See if you can guess which animal it describes.

Music

Mel's class is listening to a march. Mel's teacher asked the children what it makes them think of. Here are some words Mel wrote.

loud   happy   walking fast   lots of players

Apply Listen to the music your teacher plays for you. Make a list of words that tell about the music.

Adverbs

A. Write the adverb from each sentence.
Write **when** if the adverb tells when.
Write **where** if the adverb tells where.

1. I always feed the cat.   **3.** Today we are busy.
2. The bus turns around.   **4.** Albert lives there.

B. Write the adverbs that tell how.

5. We cheer loudly for our team.
6. Pamela writes neatly.
7. Pat quickly makes his bed.
8. Ted talks softly to the baby.

Suffixes

C. Write the words that have suffixes.

9. The sun is shining brightly.
10. This soup smells wonderful.
11. The baby bird looks helpless.
12. A broken rake is useless.
13. Deer can run swiftly.
14. Jill is always careful.

Words that Sound Alike

D. Write the two words in each sentence that sound alike.

15. He knew my coat was new.
16. You can see birds by the sea.
17. Don has two sisters, too.
18. We have four pears for you.

Paragraphs

E. Read the paragraph. Follow the directions.

The huge truck rolled along. The engine roared. The lights were shining. The bus broke down.

19. Write the sentence that tells the main idea.

20. Write a sentence that gives a detail.

21. Write a sentence that does not keep to the topic.

F. Finish the main idea below. Then write two sentences that give details about the main idea.

My favorite shoes are ___.

Checkpoint: Unit 7

A Special Invitation to Books

Cornstalks and Cannonballs

by Barbara Mitchell

In 1812, Lewes was a pretty town by the sea. Then the British attacked. The people of Lewes came up with a clever plan.

Airport

by Byron Barton

An airport is a busy and exciting place. This book shows you arriving, waiting, loading, and boarding. Are you ready for take-off?

The Quicksand Book

by Tomie de Paola

A girl falls into quicksand. She is sinking. A boy comes. He talks about quicksand. She keeps sinking. He keeps talking. This book has many facts about quicksand. It also has a surprise ending.

Dinosaur Time

by Peggy Parish

A long time ago the world was different. Dinosaurs lived everywhere. This book describes these strange creatures.

How to Find a GOOD Book

Listen to book reports for ideas.

Happy Birthday to Me

It's my birthday
And everyone says
I'm growing up.

But look—
My arms are growing down!
See my last year's sleeves?

—*Eve Merriam*

1 Commands and Exclamations

- A **command** gives an order.
  It ends with a period ⬚ . .
- An **exclamation** shows strong feeling.
  It ends with an exclamation mark ⬚! .

Get the ball.
Frisky caught it!

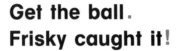

Get the ball. is a command.
It tells Frisky to do something.
Frisky caught it! is an exclamation.
It shows strong feeling.

▶ Copy the sentences below. Circle the commands.
Put a line under the exclamations.

1. What a beautiful day!
2. Bring your lunch.
3. Tell them about the picnic.
4. Our class won!
5. Get ready for the race.
6. We can't wait to start!
7. It is so exciting!

▶ Write the commands and exclamations.
Write the correct end marks.

8. What a great idea
9. Build another sand castle
10. Here comes a big wave
11. It's going to fall
12. Don't build it here
13. Move back
14. What a wonderful castle
15. Put some flags on top
16. It's so beautiful
17. Make a lake around it
18. There's a crab in the lake
19. Get the crab out
20. You did it

▶ **Apply**   Write four sentences.
Write two commands. Write two
exclamations. Use one word
below in each sentence.

bus   light   traffic   bicycle

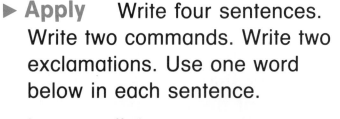

2 Writing Four Kinds of Sentences

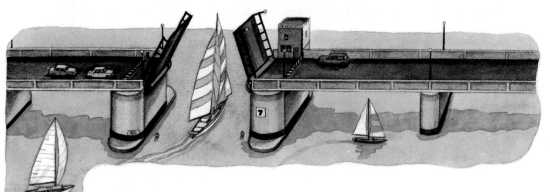

Statement	The sailboats go under the bridge.
Question	How will the ship get past?
Exclamation	What a tall ship that is!
Command	Open the bridge.

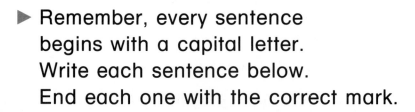

► Remember, every sentence
begins with a capital letter.
Write each sentence below.
End each one with the correct mark.

1. look at that ship
2. how beautiful that sail is
3. all of the cars wait
4. when can we go
5. don't get out of the car
6. the bridge goes up
7. what a bridge it is
8. how does it work
9. the tall ship goes past
10. did the bridge close

▶ Write sentences about the picture. The words in the box will help you.

11-12. Write two statements about the picture.

13-14. Write two questions about the picture.

15-16. Write two exclamations about the picture.

17-18. Write two commands about the picture.

noise	window	close	jam	right
street	doing	traffic	what	please
here	how	turn	workers	wait

3 Changing Meaning with Word Order

The dog chased the cat.   **The cat chased the dog.**

Remember that words in a sentence must be in an order that make sense. The meaning changes if the word order changes. Notice the words **dog** and **cat** in the sentences above. The sentences have very different meanings.

▶ Change the order of the words in dark type. Write a sentence with a different meaning.

1. **Dan** called **Luisa.**
2. **Carlos** is taller than **Sara.**
3. **The tree** fell on **the kite.**
4. **The pail** is in **the water.**
5. **Max** splashes **Andy** in the ocean.
6. **The seagull** stares at **Jeff.**
7. **My sandwich** is in **the sand.**
8. **That crab** is faster than **this snail.**

Is the bus here?
The bus is here.

Word order can change meaning.
The same words are in each sentence above.
One is a question. One is the answer.

▶ Change the word order of the sentences below.
Use the same words to write the answers.

9. Is Linda home?
10. Will it rain today?
11. Can the dog do tricks?
12. Is this book for Bob?
13. May Cara come with us?
14. Should we use this paper?
15. Are you next?
16. Was that your pet?

▶ **Apply** Write two sentences.
Make one a question.
Make one a statement.
Use the same words for both sentences.

Sentence Combining

> ● Some sentences can be combined.

A. Joan has a coat.
B. It is a new **coat.**
A. + B. Joan has a new coat.

Sentences **A** and **B** have been combined. The word **new** from sentence **B** was added to sentence **A**. It tells **what kind** of coat Joan has.

Read the sentences below.
Then tell how they can be combined.

1. We picked flowers.
   They were **pretty** flowers.

2. Mike won the prize.
   It was the **first** prize.

3. This is a school.
   It is a **big** school.

4. That is a pig.
   It is a **cute** pig.

C. Pablo spoke.

D. He spoke softly.

C + D. Pablo spoke softly.

Sentences **C** and **D** have been combined. The word **softly** from sentence **D** was added to sentence **C**. It tells **how** Pablo spoke.

Read the sentences below.
Then tell how they can be combined.

5. The girls sang.
They sang **loudly**.

6. Tara ran.
She ran **quickly**.

Read the sentences below.
Then write the combined sentences.

7. David told a joke.
It was a **funny** joke.

8. We had a cat.
It was a **black** cat.

9. Mrs. Wong smiled.
She smiled **kindly.**

10. The class watched the teacher.
They watched him **carefully**.

4 Parts of a Book

When you open a book, you may see a page
that looks like one of these.

The **title** is the name of the book.
The **author** is the person who wrote the book.

▶ Look at the pages above.
Answer these questions.

1. What is the title of the book about cats
and dogs?

2. Who is the author of the book about cats
and dogs?

3. What is the title of the book about jungle cats?

4. Who is the author of the book about jungle cats?

The **table of contents** tells what is in the book. It tells on what page each part begins.

▶ Look at the table of contents above. Answer these questions.

5. What is the title of the first part of the book?

6. On what page does the third part of the book begin?

7. You want to find out what was learned from later moon walks. What page would you turn to?

▶ **Apply** Look at the first page of the Table of Contents in this book. Answer these questions.

8. On what page does a lesson on questions begin?

9. On what page could you learn about taking a message?

5 Parts of a Book Report

A book report is a way to share a book you have read. When you write a book report:

- Write the title.
  Begin the first, last, and all important words with a capital letter.
- Write the name of the author.
- Tell what the book is about. Tell the name of the most important person in the book.
- Tell one or two things that happen in the book. Do not tell how it ends.
- Tell what you think about the book. If you like it, tell why.

▶ Read Linda's book report.

Linda Dino

Title Tye May and the Magic Brush

Author Molly Garret Bang

This book is about Tye May. She has a magic brush. The things she paints come to life. I think this book is exciting. Read it to find out how she used her brush.

▶ Choose a book you like. Then finish this book report. Use a form like the one below for your report. Use as many lines as you need for each part.

Name ___

Title ___

Author ___

This book is about ___.

I think this book is ___.

6 Sharing a Book

You can tell your classmates about books you enjoy. Here are some ideas for sharing a book.

Paper Bag Book Report
Write the title and author of your book on a paper bag. Decorate the bag with pictures of the story characters.

T-Shirt Book Report
Cut a T-shirt out of paper. Write the title and author of your book on the T-shirt. You can draw pictures on your T-shirt, too.

Milk Carton Book Report
Draw pictures for the beginning, middle, and end of your book. Glue one picture to each side of a milk carton. On the fourth side, write the title and author of your book.

▶ Share a book with the class.

7 Using the Library

A **library** has hundreds of books in it. If you have a **library card**, you can borrow the books.

Your library has **fiction** and **nonfiction** books. Fiction books are about people and things that are made up. Nonfiction books are about real people and things.

A library also has **magazines**. It may have **records** and **films**. It may have a **display case** that shows special collections.

▶ Complete the sentences about a library.

1. You must have a ___ ___ to borrow books.
2. ___ books are about people and things that are made up.
3. ___ books are about real people and things.
4. A ___ ___ shows special collections.

**Writing
Project**

8 Writing a Book Report

A book report can tell other readers about a good book. You can write a book report to display in the school library.

1. Prewriting

▶ Think of your favorite books. Which book has a main character that you really like? Choose that book for your report. Draw a picture of the main character. Show your favorite part of the book.

The Bear

► Pretend you are the main character of the book. Have a partner interview you. Answer these questions. Answer other questions your partner wants to ask.

- Who are you?

- What happens to you in your favorite part of the book?

- Why should everyone read your story?

- How do you feel in the book?

2. Writing

► Write the title and the author of your book. Now write about your book. Pretend you are the main character. Tell what the main character would say about your book. At the end, sign the character's name.

3. Revising

▶ Discuss your book report
with your interview partner.

• Are my words in an order that
makes sense?

• Can I combine sentences?

Read Evan's book report. He combined two
sentences when he revised.

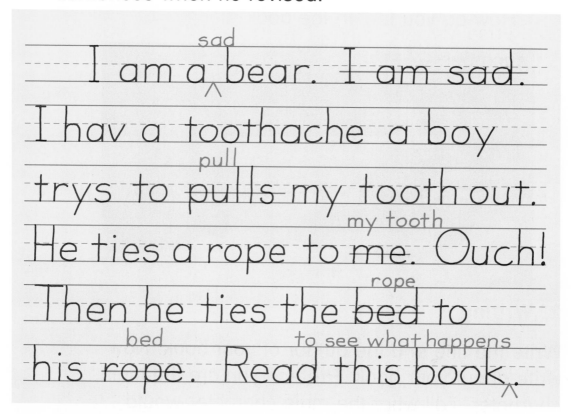

I am a ∧sad bear. ~~I am sad.~~

I hav a toothache a boy

trys to ~~pulls~~ pull my tooth out.

He ties a rope to me my tooth. Ouch!

Then he ties the ~~bed~~ rope to

his ~~rope~~ bed. Read this book∧ to see what happens.

▶ Now revise your book report. Use the
revising marks to make changes.

4. Publishing

▶ Proofread your book report. Use the proofreading marks to make corrections. These questions will help you proofread.

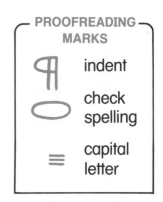

- Did I indent the first word?

- Did I spell each word correctly?

- Did I begin each sentence with a capital letter?

- Did I use the correct mark at the end of each sentence?

> I (hav) a toothache. a boy (trys) to pulls my tooth out.
>
> *have*   *tries*   *pull*

▶ Make a book poster. Hang your poster in the library so that everyone can read about a good book.

A Book Jacket

Make a book jacket about your favorite book.

1. Get a large piece of construction paper.
2. Hold it sideways. Put one side edge over the other. Make a neat fold in the center. Open the paper, and fold each side edge in.
3. Write the title of your book on the front. Write the author's name under the title.
4. Draw a picture of some people or an event from the book.
5. Write a short paragraph that tells what the book is about. Put it on one of the flaps you folded.

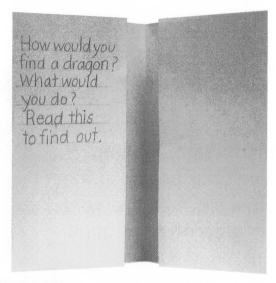

Mathematics

What kind of books do your classmates like best? Interview your classmates to find out. Ask each classmate to choose a favorite kind of book.

books about animals
books about people
books about make-believe things
books about funny things

After your interviews, make a table like the one below. List the kinds of books. How many people chose each kind of book? Write the total number for each kind of book.

Favorite Kinds of Books

Sentences

A. Copy the sentences. Circle each command. Put a line under each exclamation.

1. How tired I am!
Go to bed now.

2. Read us a story.
What a good book!

3. Look for your shoes.
I found them!

4. How heavy this bag is!
Put it on the table.

5. What a busy day!
Finish your work.

6. Make a funny face.
How silly he looks!

B. Write the sentences. Begin each one with a capital letter. Write the correct end mark.

7. open the car door

8. how dark it is

9. we clean our desks

10. where are you going

C. Write four kinds of sentences about summer.

11. Write a statement.
12. Write a question.
13. Write a command.
14. Write an exclamation.

D. Write the words in a different order to answer each question.

15. Will Jeff come?
16. Can Lisa skate?
17. Is Ted here?
18. Should we hurry?
19. Is it time to meet Beth?

Finding Information

E. Write the correct answer for each clue. Use the words in the box.

nonfiction book
author
table of contents
title
fiction book

20. It tells what is in a book.
21. It is about real people and things.
22. It is about made-up people and things.
23. It is a person who writes books.
24. It is the name of a book.

Sentences

A. Find the sentences and write them.

1. **a.** A blue boat   **b.** Sue rows the boat.
2. **a.** We pick berries.   **b.** A bowl of berries
3. **a.** The traffic light   **b.** The light is red.
4. **a.** I eat breakfast.   **b.** Eggs for breakfast

B. Copy the sentences. Circle each command. Put a line under each exclamation.

5. Put on your bathing suit.
6. How cool the water is!
7. Bring your pail and shovel.
8. What a big wave that is!

C. Write each sentence. Begin each one with a capital letter. Write the correct end mark.

9. the rain has stopped
10. do you want to go outside
11. what a big puddle that is
12. look at the rainbow

Nouns

D. Write the word that means more than one.

13. foot   feet   **15.** cage   cages
14. hills   hill   **16.** men   man

E. Write each name, title, or special day correctly.

17. friday   **19.** flag day
18. puss in boots   **20.** dr jill hall

Pronouns

F. Write pronouns for the words in ( ). Use **He**, **It**, **We**, or **They**.

21. (Jim and I) dance.   **23.** (Doug) is friendly.
22. (The candle) burns.   **24.** (Bev and Pam) skate.

G. Write the correct word in ( ).

25. Max and (I, me) ride horses.
26. Terry told (I, me) a secret.
27. I need (a, an) empty box.
28. Gail saw (a, an) baby bird.

Verbs

H. Write the correct verb in ( ).

29. Sandy (is, are) in the school band.
30. Frank (have, has) a clown suit.
31. Claudia (paint, painted) yesterday.
32. Patty and I (know, knows) the answer.
33. Ed (enjoy, enjoys) his swimming lessons.
34. My twin sisters (look, looks) alike.

I. Write the verb that tells about the past.

35. run   ran
36. took   take
37. went   go

38. do   did
39. give   gave
40. came   come

Adjectives

J. Write the words that tell how many or what kind.

41. Tim needs two crayons.
42. Monkeys make funny faces.
43. Kara likes old movies.
44. A spider has eight legs.

K. Add **-er** or **-est** to the words in ( ).
Then write them for the sentences.

45. The blue coat is (warm) than the red one.
46. The green coat is the (warm) of all.
47. My desk is (small) than your desk.
48. That desk is the (small) of all.

Adverbs

L. Write the adverbs. Write **when** if the adverb tells when. Write **where** if the adverb tells where.

49. I never eat snacks.

50. The race ends here.

51. The birds sing now.

52. My tent falls down.

M. Write the adverbs that tell how.

53. Mary works carefully.
54. The parade moves slowly.
55. The rain starts suddenly.
56. Mr. Collins smiles kindly.

Acknowledgments continued from page ii

Permissions: We wish to thank the following authors, publishers, agents, corporations, and individuals for their permission to reprint copyrighted materials. Page 5: "What Do You Do?" from *Making Music Your Own, K.* Copyright © 1966 by Silver Burdett Company. Reprinted by permission of Silver Burdett Company. Page 24: Cover illustration by Ray Cruz from *Alexander and the Terrible, Horrible, No Good, Very Bad Day* by Judith Viorst. Illustration copyright © 1972 Ray Cruz. Reprinted with the permission of Atheneum Publishers, Inc. Page 35: "Open House," first and last stanzas, by Aileen Fisher. Reprinted by permission of the author. Page 41: The first stanza of the poem "Run in the Rain" by Aileen Fisher. Reprinted by permission of the author. Page 61: "Somersaults" from *Rainy Rainy Saturday* by Jack Prelutsky. Copyright © 1980 by Jack Prelutsky. Reprinted by permission of William Morrow & Company, Inc. Page 65: "Peeking In" by Aileen Fisher. Reprinted by permission of the author. Page 74: *The Snowy Day* by Ezra Jack Keats. Copyright © 1962 by Ezra Jack Keats. Reprinted by permission of Viking Penguin, Inc., and The Bodley Head, London, England. Page 97: "Tugs" from *I Go A-Traveling* by James S. Tippett. Reprinted by permission of Harper & Row, Publishers, Inc. Page 110: "Catch a Little Rhyme" from *Catch a Little Rhyme* by Eve Merriam. All rights reserved. Reprinted by permission of Marian Reiner for the author. "Skyscraper" from *Alligator Pie* © 1974 by Dennis Lee. Reprinted by permission of Macmillan of Canada, a Division of Canada Publishing Corp. Page 111: "Little Snail" from *Poems By a Little Girl* by Hilda Conkling. "Thorn Song" from *The Prancing Pony, Nursery Poems from Japan.* Adapted by Charlotte B. DeForest. © 1967 by John Weatherhill, Inc. Page 112: "The Shell" from *Far and Few* by David McCord. Copyright 1934 by David McCord. Used by permission of Little, Brown & Company, Inc. "Marisol" from *The Tamarindo Puppy* by Charlotte Pomerantz. Copyright © 1980 by Charlotte Pomerantz. By permission of Greenwillow Books, a Division of William Morrow & Company, Inc. Page 113: "Solitude" by A. A. Milne from *Now We Are Six.* Copyright 1927 by E. P. Dutton, Inc., a Division of The New American Library, Inc. "The Bird's Nest" by John Drinkwater. Page 114: "I'd Like to Be a Lighthouse" from *Taxis and Toadstools* by Rachel Field. Copyright 1926 Doubleday & Company, Inc., and William Heinemann, Ltd., London, England. Reprinted by permission. "I Like It When It's Mizzly" from *I Like Weather* by Aileen Fisher (Thomas Y. Crowell Company, Publishers) Copyright © 1963 by Aileen Fisher. Reprinted by permission of Harper & Row, Publishers, Inc. Page 116: "Pick Me Up" from *Laughing Time: Nonsense Poems* by William Jay Smith, published by Delacorte Press, 1980. Copyright © 1953, 1955, 1956, 1957, 1959, 1968, 1974, 1980. Reprinted by permission of Delacorte Press/Seymour and William Jay Smith. 118: "Ayii, ayii, ayii..." from *Songs of the Dream People* by James Houston. Page 120: "Some One" by Walter de la Mare. Reprinted by permission of The Society of Authors. Representative of the Literary Trustees of Walter de la Mare. Page 121: "Crick! Crack!" from *Blackberry Ink* by Eve Merriam. All rights reserved. Reprinted by permission of Marian Reiner for the author. Page 133: "Thoughts in Bed" from *Open the Door: Rhymes for Children* by Marion Edey. Copyright © 1949 by Marion Edey and Dorothy Grider. Reprinted with the permission of Charles Scribner's Sons. Page 136: Front cover by Donald Carrick of *More Alex and the Cat* by Helen V. Griffith. Copyright © 1983 by Donald Carrick. Reprinted by permission of Greenwillow Books, a Division of William Morrow & Company, Inc. *Sing a Song of Sixpence* pictures by Tracey Campbell Pearson. Pictures copyright © 1985 by Tracey Campbell Pearson. Reproduced by permission of the publisher, Dial Books for Young Readers. *A Special Trade* by Sally Wittman, pictures by Karen Gundersheimer. © 1978 by Harper & Row, Publishers, Inc. Reprinted by permission of the publisher. Page 161: "Tails" from *Whispers and Other Poems* by Myra Cohn Livingston. Reprinted by permission of Marian Reiner for the author. Page 174: Entire text of *Emma* by Wendy Kesselman. Copyright © 1980 by Wendy Kesselman. Reprinted by permission of Doubleday & Company, Inc. Page 199: "My Dog" by Lois Lenski. Used by permission of The Lois Lenski Foundation, Inc. Page 223: "Happy Birthday to Me" from *Catch a Little Rhyme* by Eve Merriam. All rights reserved. Reprinted by permission of Marian Reiner for the author. Page 235: *Momo's Kitten* by Taro Yashima. © 1961 by Viking Press. Used by permission. From *Frog and Toad Are Friends* by Arnold Lobel. Used by permission of Harper & Row, Publishers, Inc. From *Where the Wild Things Are* by Maurice Sendak. Used by permission of Harper & Row, Publishers, Inc. Page 236: *Amelia Bedelia* by Peggy Parish, illustrated by Fritz Siebel. Published by Harper & Row, Publishers, Inc. Used by permission of the publisher. *Make Way for Ducklings* by Robert McCloskey. © 1971, 1969 by Puffin Books. Used by permission of Viking Penguin, Inc.

250

Contents

GRAMMAR HANDBOOK

COMPOSITION HANDBOOK

WORD FINDER

WRITING AND THE COMPUTER

Sentences

sentence ● A **sentence** tells a complete idea.
It begins with a capital letter.   page 6

Horses run fast.

statement ● End a **statement** with a period ⌈.⌉. page 8

Monkeys have long tails.

question ● End a **question** with a question mark ⌈?⌉.
page 10

Did you paint this?

MORE PRACTICE   Sentences

A. Find the sentences and write them.

1. **a.** My friend Sally
   b. My friend visits me.

2. **a.** Ducks swim in the pond.
   b. in the pond and the lake

B. Find the questions and write them.

3. Can we play here?
4. Now we will eat lunch.
5. My dog sleeps a lot.
6. Where is your bike?
7. Did the rain stop?
8. Jim walks home.

Nouns

noun ● A **noun** names a person, place, or thing.   page 36

> **My aunt has trees in her yard.**

● Many words add **-s** to mean **more than one**.   page 39

> **ball + s = balls**

● Some words change to mean **more than one**.   page 40

> **one tooth   two teeth**

MORE PRACTICE   Nouns

A. Copy the sentences. Circle the nouns.

1. The boys run in the park.
2. Cars drive down the street.
3. My sister made a kite.
4. A turtle is on the rock now.

B. Write a word that means more than one for each noun below.

5. dog	**8.** foot	**11.** girl
6. hat	**9.** sled	**12.** man
7. road	**10.** river	**13.** child

Verbs

verb ● A word that shows action
is a **verb**. page 62

Fish swim in water.

● Add **-s** to a verb to tell about
one person or thing. page 64

One frog hops.   Two frogs hop.

● Many verbs that tell about the past
end with **-ed**. page 65

Now I jump.   Yesterday I jumped.

MORE PRACTICE   Verbs

A. Copy the sentences. Circle the verbs.
  1. I sing with my friends.
  2. My dog barks and runs.
  3. We eat eggs and toast.
  4. Lee rides a bike.

B. Write the verbs below in
the past time.

  5. We climb up the hill.
  6. They plant the seeds.
  7. Joe and I march in the band.
  8. My friends play tag.

Adjectives

adjective ● An **adjective** tells more about
   a noun.   page 98

   I have shoes.   I have red shoes.

● Add **-er** to an adjective to compare
   two persons, places, or things.   page 104

   Jill is taller than Sue.

● Add **-est** to an adjective to compare
   three or more persons, places,
   or things.   page 104

   Jack is the tallest of all.

MORE PRACTICE   Adjectives

A. Copy the sentences. Circle the
   adjectives.

   1. We made funny pictures.
   2. We have two books.
   3. Joan has blue mittens.
   4. They like large boats.

B. Add **-er** or **-est** to each word in (   ).

   5. I am (old)___ than John.
   6. Bill is the (old)___ of all.

Nouns

capital ● The names of people, pets, and places
letters begin with capital letters.   page 134

Kim Anton   **Frisky**   **Kansas**

● Titles for people begin with capital
letters. Most titles end with a period.
page 135

Mr.   **Mrs.**   **Ms.**   **Dr.**   **Miss**

● Begin the first, last, and all important
words in a book title with capital
letters.   page 136

Sam and the Owl   **Hunting for Frogs**

● The names of days, months, holidays,
and special days begin with capital
letters.   pages 137, 138

Friday   **June**   **Flag Day**

MORE PRACTICE Nouns

1. sue rowe   **3.** denver   **5.** a big day
2. puff   **4.** mr lee   **6.** tuesday

Verbs

special verb forms ● Some verbs that tell about the past do not add **-ed**. pages 162–167

Now	In the Past
is	was
are	were
have	had
come	came
run	ran
give	gave
take	took
do	did
go	went

MORE PRACTICE Verbs

Make the sentences below tell about the past. Write the new sentences.

1. That is a good story.
2. We run in the park.
3. My friends go to the library.
4. Karen and Rob take a ride.
5. They come to my party.

Adverbs

adverb ● An **adverb** tells more about a verb.

page 200

We write nicely.

MORE PRACTICE   Adverbs

A. Write the adverbs that tell **when**.

    1. John painted yesterday.
    2. You never spill anything.
    3. Today Lisa ran in a race.
    4. My dog always finds me.

B. Write the adverbs that tell **where**.

    5. Please put down your books.
    6. Jim and I wait here.
    7. My kite went up.
    8. Look around before you cross.

C. Write the adverbs that tell **how**.

    9. Trees grow slowly.
   10. She carefully cleans her brush.
   11. Maria sings quietly.
   12. The butterfly landed softly.

Commands and Exclamations

command • A **command** gives an order.
It ends with a period [.]. page 224

Tie your shoelace.

exclamation • An **exclamation** shows strong feeling.
It ends with an exclamation mark [!].
page 224

What a surprise this is!

MORE PRACTICE Commands and Exclamations

A. Write **command** or **exclamation** for each sentence.

1. Put that away.
2. There was a huge storm!
3. We found the hidden treasure!
4. Close the door.

B. Write the commands and exclamations. Write the correct end marks.

5. Come home now
6. Get ready to go
7. I loved the play
8. I can't believe it
9. The robot works
10. Tell me a riddle

Friendly Letter and Envelope

friendly letter
- A friendly letter has five parts: the **date**, **greeting**, **body**, **closing**, and **signature**.   page 148

comma
- Use a **comma** $\boxed{,}$ between the day and year and after the greeting and the closing.   page 149

return address
- The **return address** tells who is sending the letter. page 151

address

The **address** tells who will receive the letter.
page 151

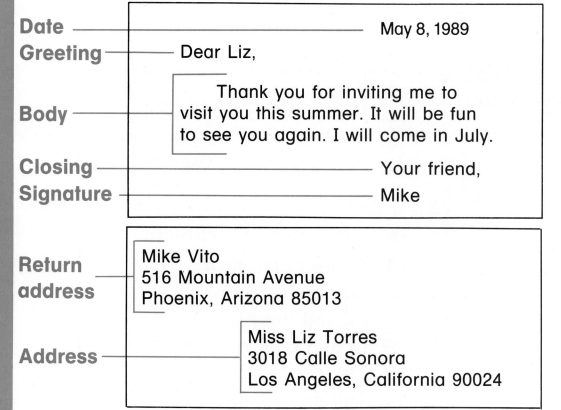

Date — May 8, 1989

Greeting — Dear Liz,

Body —
    Thank you for inviting me to visit you this summer. It will be fun to see you again. I will come in July.

Closing — Your friend,

Signature — Mike

Return address —
Mike Vito
516 Mountain Avenue
Phoenix, Arizona 85013

Address —
Miss Liz Torres
3018 Calle Sonora
Los Angeles, California 90024

Paragraphs

paragraph ● A **paragraph** is a group of sentences about one main idea.   page 208

indented ● The first word in a paragraph is **indented**. page 208

Main —————— <u>Larimer Park is a wonderful place.</u>
idea It has picnic tables and grills. There is a lake with a dock and rowboats. Near the lake there is a playground.

Book Report

book report ● A **book report** is a way to share a book you have read. page 234

Name ___

Title ___

Author ___

   This book is about ___ .

I think this book is ___ .

Revising and Proofreading Marks

Use these marks to make changes when you write.

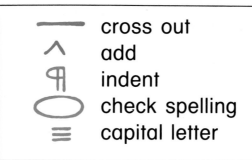

—	cross out
∧	add
¶	indent
◯	check spelling
≡	capital letter

Proofreading Checklist

Proofread your writing before you make a final copy. Use the proofreading checklist. Ask yourself each question. Check **yes** or **no** for each one. Use the proofreading marks to make your corrections.

Questions	Yes	No
1. Did I spell each word correctly?		
2. Did I begin each sentence with a capital letter?		
3. Did I use the correct mark at the end of each sentence?		
4. Did I indent the first word of a paragraph?		
5. Did I use my best handwriting?		

Word Finder

Main Entry Words

animal 264	**cook** 267	**happy** 269	**put** 271
		hot 270	
bad 264	**fruit** 267		**sad** 272
big 265			**say** 272
break 265	**get** 268	**little** 270	
building 266	**go** 268	**look** 270–271	
	good 269		**vegetable** 273
cold 266	**ground** 269	**make** 271	**well** 273

Synonyms for Main Entry Words

apartment house 266	Earth 269	lay 271	school 266
apple 267	easily 273	lettuce 273	see 270
awful 264	elephant 264	library 266	set 271
	excellent 269	lion 264	shape 271
bake 267	excellently 273	lonely 272	short 270
banana 267	explode 265	loud 265	shout 272
boil 267			sick 264
build 271	fish 264	miserable 272	smash 265
burning 270	floor 269		sorry 272
buy 268	fly 268	onion 273	spicy 270
	frosty 266	orange 267	stare 271
call 272	fry 267		
carefully 273		peach 267	
carrot 273	giraffe 264	peek 270	tear 265
catch 268	glad 269	place 271	tiny 270
cheerful 269	grill 267	pleasant 269	
cool 266		potato 273	walk 268
crack 265	house 266		warm 270
create 271	huge 265	quiet 270	watch 271
			whisper 272
dangerous 264	icy 266	recite 272	win 268
dirt 269	important 265	ride 268	
dog 264	jolly 269	right 269	
	jump 268	run 268	young 270

WORD FINDER

animal a living creature.
A crocodile is a long <u>animal</u>.

dog a pet that barks and that has four legs and a tail.
My <u>dog</u> can sit up and shake hands.

elephant a large animal with a long trunk, floppy ears, tusks, and four legs.
I fed peanuts to that <u>elephant</u>.

fish an animal that has fins, gills, and a tail, and that lives in water.
A <u>fish</u> lives in fresh or salt water.

giraffe a very tall animal that has four long legs and a long neck.
The <u>giraffe</u> can peek over the high fence.

lion a large member of the cat family.
The <u>lion</u> hunts for its food.

bad not good.
I have a <u>bad</u> cold.

awful very bad or unpleasant.
The burnt food smelled <u>awful</u>.

dangerous not safe.
We won't drive on a <u>dangerous</u> road.

sick in bad health.
When I feel <u>sick</u>, I go to bed.

big large in size.
The big plane flew away.

huge unusually large.
The huge cloud blocked the sun.

important of much value.
The mayor has an important job.

loud easy to hear.
The drums made a loud sound.

break to cause something to come apart.
The vase will break if you drop it.

crack to damage something without
having it fall apart.
Ice can crack when you walk on it
if it is not thick.

explode to blow apart.
The balloon will explode if you
blow too much air into it.

smash to break into many small pieces.
A glass will smash if you drop it.

tear to rip something apart.
Did you tear the paper into two pieces?

WORD FINDER

building	something having walls, floors, and a roof, where people live or work. That <u>building</u> is three floors high.
apartment house	a large building where many families live. Six families live in my <u>apartment house</u>.
house	a building where a family lives. My family lives in a yellow <u>house</u>.
library	a building with many books. Every Saturday Tony goes to the <u>library</u> to take out books.
school	a building with classrooms, pupils, and teachers. That <u>school</u> is on Elm Street.
cold	having a very low temperature. When the weather gets <u>cold</u>, I sneeze.
cool	not completely cold. The autumn wind is <u>cool</u>.
frosty	covered with frost. Sometimes when it is cold, the grass looks white and <u>frosty</u>.
icy	like ice. An <u>icy</u> wind blew the snow into drifts.

cook   to prepare food with heat.
We <u>cook</u> our dinner every night.

bake   to cook in an oven.
The house smells wonderful when we <u>bake</u> bread.

boil   to cook in water.
We <u>boil</u> beets in a pot.

fry   to cook in fat or oil.
Let's <u>fry</u> the fish.

grill   to cook over an open fire.
We <u>grill</u> hamburgers in the summer.

fruit   the part of a plant that has seeds and may usually be eaten.
I love to eat <u>fruit</u> in the summer.

apple   a round red, green, or yellow fruit that grows on trees.
This <u>apple</u> is sweet and juicy.

banana   a long, curved fruit with thick yellow skin.
It is fun to peel a <u>banana</u>.

orange   a round fruit with a thick skin.
The juice is from this <u>orange</u>.

peach   a sweet, round fruit with fuzzy skin.
I watched a <u>peach</u> grow on our tree.

WORD FINDER

WORD FINDER

get	to own or to have something. John will <u>get</u> a dog for his birthday.
buy	to own after paying for something. I earned money to <u>buy</u> this book.
catch	to capture something by trapping. I can <u>catch</u> a ball with my mitt.
win	to get something in a contest. Only one person can <u>win</u> the prize.
go	to move to or from something. We <u>go</u> to the store.
fly	to move in the air using wings. I saw a jet <u>fly</u> in the sky.
jump	to leap up or leap over something. The horses <u>jump</u> over the fence.
ride	to move in or on something. We <u>ride</u> in a train to the city.
run	to go faster than walking. We can <u>run</u> until our legs hurt.
walk	to move one foot in front of the other. When I <u>walk</u>, I look at everything.

good   pleasing, right, or proper.
Dan is a <u>good</u> boy to help his brother.

excellent   very, very good.
Jane is an <u>excellent</u> swimmer,
because she practices every day.

pleasant   nice or enjoyable.
We had a <u>pleasant</u> time at the zoo.

right   correct or proper.
It is <u>right</u> to tell the truth.

ground   the surface of the earth.
We planted flowers in the <u>ground</u>.

dirt   loose, top layer of the ground.
The wind blew <u>dirt</u> into our house.

Earth   the planet we live on.
<u>Earth</u> is the third planet away from
the sun.

floor   the part of a room we walk on.
There is a red rug on the <u>floor</u>.

happy   feeling well and pleased.
I am <u>happy</u> when I visit my grandma.

cheerful   full of good feeling.
Joan is always smiling and <u>cheerful</u>.

jolly   very, very happy.
Tom is so <u>jolly</u> he laughs all the time.

glad   happy about something.
Mary was <u>glad</u> you came to visit her.

WORD FINDER

hot	having a very high temperature. The sun makes the sidewalk <u>hot</u>.
burning	hot enough to cause pain. Anne's <u>burning</u> skin feels painful.
spicy	having a hot or peppery taste. This is a <u>spicy</u> sauce.
warm	not quite hot. The spring air feels <u>warm</u>.
little	not of great size. Tom's balloon was <u>little</u>.
quiet	hard to hear. Kevin sang in a <u>quiet</u> voice.
short	not very tall. My baby brother is too <u>short</u> to reach the shelf.
tiny	very, very small. The <u>tiny</u> bug sat on my finger.
young	not having many years. A <u>young</u> cat is a kitten.
look	to see something with your eyes. <u>Look</u> at the shooting star!
peek	to look at something secretly. I can <u>peek</u> at the chipmunk from here.
see	to be able to look at something. Cindy can <u>see</u> the bus coming.

look (continued)

stare	to keep looking at something for a long time, without blinking. We <u>stare</u> at the fish and the fish <u>stare</u> at us.
watch	to observe something for a while. I like to <u>watch</u> the birds fly south.
make	to cause something to be or to happen. Sally can <u>make</u> lunch for herself.
build	to construct something from materials. We will <u>build</u> a clubhouse with wood, nails, and shingles.
create	to make something new. Can you <u>create</u> a new game?
shape	to give form to something. Nancy can <u>shape</u> clay into a turtle.
put	to move something to a place. Bill <u>put</u> his bike in the garage.
lay	to put something down. <u>Lay</u> the mat in front of the door.
place	To move something to a certain spot. <u>Place</u> this dish on top of the others.
set	to arrange something somewhere for a reason. We <u>set</u> the seedlings out in the garden.

WORD FINDER

sad	unhappy. I was <u>sad</u> when my dog ran away.
lonely	alone and sad. Kathy felt <u>lonely</u> when her best friend moved away.
miserable	very, very unhappy. Josh was <u>miserable</u> until his sick puppy got better.
sorry	sad about something that was said or done. I was <u>sorry</u> I broke the plate.

say	to put into words. I always <u>say</u> what I think.
call	to address yourself to someone. Will you <u>call</u> my name next?
recite	to speak from memory. We <u>recite</u> "The Pledge of Allegiance" every day.
shout	to say in a loud voice. Conductors always <u>shout</u> "All aboard!"
whisper	to say in a very quiet voice. How softly can you <u>whisper</u> the clue?

vegetable a plant whose roots, leaves, stems, or flowers can be eaten.
Celery is a green <u>vegetable</u>.

carrot a long, thin, orange root.
I like to eat a raw <u>carrot</u>.

lettuce a plant with crisp green leaves.
Scot puts lots of <u>lettuce</u> in his salad.

onion a bulb of the lily family.
Do you cry when you cut an <u>onion</u>?

potato a vegetable with a brown, yellow, or orange skin that grows underground.
A <u>potato</u> can be baked, boiled, fried, or mashed.

well in a good way.
The party is going <u>well</u>.

carefully with care.
Todd climbed down <u>carefully</u>.

easily without trouble.
We <u>easily</u> followed the map.

excellently very, very well.
You played that song <u>excellently</u>.

Writing and the Computer

How Do You Write?

Some children draw a picture first. Then they write a story to go with it.

After you write your story, you may want to change it. You make the changes with a pencil on your paper.

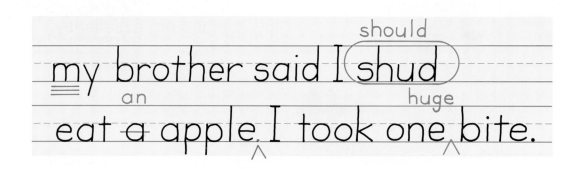

Another Way to Write

Some computer programs have pictures you can arrange on the screen. You can get ideas for stories when you put your picture together. You can

- choose pictures.
- change pictures.
- move parts of the picture around.

THE CURIOUS COW
Dillie was a farmcow. She had always lilved on a farm. One day she decidded to see something else. So she set of for the city.

Then you can write a story about your picture. As you write, you can

- add words.
- change words.
- take words out.

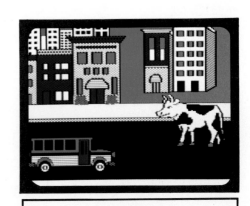

THE CURIOUS COW

Dillie was a farm cow. She had always lived on a farm.
One day she decided to see something else. So she set off for the city.

You can print your story and picture, or save them on a disk.

When You Write with a Computer

Loading a Program

Computer programs come on a **disk**. The disk has to be put into the **disk drive**. Then you will see the program begin to work on the **screen**.

disk

disk drive on

disk drive

Using a Program

You will see directions on the screen. They tell you how to use the program. You will also see a **menu**. You can choose the part of the program you want to use from the menu.

Welcome
to
Silver Burdett
& Ginn
English

computer

Saving Your Work

After you use the program, you may want to save your work. If you plan to do more to it another time, you can save it on a disk. If you have a printer, you can make a copy for yourself.

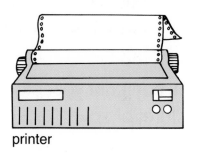

printer

Ideas to Try

There are many ways you can write with computer programs. You can use a computer to write your Writing Projects. Here are some other ideas to try.

Making Lists

You can keep a list of

- ideas for stories. When you need an idea, look at your list. Add to your list when you get new ideas.

- stories you write, and the date you write them. This can be a Table of Contents for your Writing Folder.

- books you read. You could keep another list of books you want to read.

Making Forms

You can make up your own form for

- book reports. Print some copies of your form. Use it when you want to share a book.

- a journal. Print copies of your form. Use it for your journal entries.

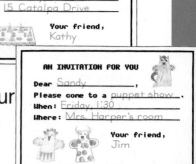

INDEX

INDEX